D1174416

Stop Looking and Listen

Il y a cinq règnes: le règne minéral, le règne
végétal, le règne animal, le règne humain et le
règne chrétien . . . Et il n'y a pas moins d'écart
et il n'y a pas moins d'avènement et il n'y a
pas moins de discontinuité du troisième au
quatrième, et du quatrième au cinquième,
qu'entre n'importe lesquels des trois autres.

—CHARLES PÉGUY, *Pensées*, XIV, 9
(Librairie Gallimard, Paris. By permission
of the publisher and Madame Péguy.)

CHAD WALSH

>>>>>>>>>>>>>>>>>>>> <<<<<<<<<<<<<<<<<<<<

STOP LOOKING

and

LISTEN

An Invitation to the Christian Life

HARPER & BROTHERS · *Publishers* · NEW YORK · LONDON

For

William Oliver Johnson

Beloit, Wisconsin

. . . CRISTES LOORE AND HIS APOSTLES TWELVE
HE TAUGHTE, BUT FIRST HE FOLWED IT HYMSELVE.

Contents

Foreword

I wish I could mention here all the people who have given me ideas for this book, but the list would run into hundreds. I would have to ransack my memories of the long evenings of talk in Ann Arbor and Arlington, and recall casual encounters in many other places. And if I tried to make acknowledgment to everyone who has unwittingly helped me I would embarrass many of my best friends. It has often happened with me (and I think this is a common experience) that I was not sure of my own opinions until I heard opposite or divergent views so well defended that I was driven to do some hard thinking of my own. Probably my agnostic, Bahá'í, and Renardan friends would not relish seeing their names listed as "influences" in a work which is candidly designed as a recruiting pamphlet for Christianity. They have helped me nonetheless, and though I omit their names my gratitude to them is very great.

Three Christian friends exerted a deep influence on me, albeit of a delayed-reaction kind. Madame Agnes L. Herwig, who was my professor of French and German at Marion College, and Miss May Scherer, dean of the same school, tried with no visible success to win me from atheism, but their words—and still more the examples of their lives—spoke to me years afterwards. My good friend, the Reverend George

B. Owen of Bellows Falls, Vermont, never made any conscious attempt to convert me, but his casual remarks set me thinking—also years later.

The reader in quest of written influences will detect traces of two Anglicans, a Roman Catholic, and a Protestant. The first Anglican is Mr. C. S. Lewis, whose books I have devoured both for the sheer joy of reading them and for the penetrating understanding he displays of "just plain Christianity." The writings of Dr. Bernard Iddings Bell, the other Anglican, showed me the ultimate philosophic results of thoroughgoing agnosticism, and the irreconcilable conflict between historic Christianity and the watered-down faith which he so aptly terms "Neo-Christianity." The reflections on the religious significance of creative work (Chapter 9 of this book) were in part suggested by his baccalaureate address, "How to Live in the Twentieth Century," which was delivered at Beloit College in 1946. I am also grateful to him for the personal encouragement and helpful advice he gave me while I was writing this book; he cannot, however, be held responsible for anything I say. The Roman Catholic, G. K. Chesterton, was by all odds one of the sanest thinkers of his time. To him I am indebted for the realization that paradoxes are not a mere exercise of wit: truth itself often consists of the simultaneous existence of two concepts that seemingly contradict each other, and of all religions Christianity is the most paradoxical. Finally, I have been greatly stimulated by the Protestant, Professor Reinhold Niebuhr. His books provide a searching analysis of the relation between Christianity, society, and political and economic systems.

My views on decentralization (Chapter 9) have been much influenced by my friend, Professor James F. Rettger of the University of Michigan. I have been privileged to read in manuscript form a book of his in which he describes an imaginary country whose social system is planned in such a way as to prevent large accumulations of economic power, whether private or governmental. The publication of Professor

Rettger's book should do much to dispel the spirit of fatalism which has stultified most social thinking in recent years. It presents a third alternative to the dreadful "either-or" of "either Capitalism à la Henry Ford or Communism à la Stalin."

My only excuse for writing this treatise on Christianity is that I had the advantage of being an ardent atheist from the time I first began to think about religion. I had a head start on all my friends who renounced their religion when they dissected their first dogfish in biology laboratory. I saw Christianity with fresh eyes when I finally grew willing to look at it. No born-and-bred Christian can realize how alluring Christianity is when you are on the outside looking in.

I fancy that my experience will be repeated on a more extensive scale a few generations from now, when the shallowness of secular philosophy has had sufficient time to reveal itself with appalling clarity. Meanwhile, I hope that anyone who feels himself in revolt against the dead-end habits of thought which have gripped most thinking Americans for the last fifty years will find this book of use as a brief statement of an alternative way of looking at life. It is intended for the discontented and rebellious: for men and women who are unwilling to absorb their opinions spongelike from the intellectual atmosphere about them.

I believe that my presentation of Christian beliefs contains nothing new. My intention was not to advance startling theological novelties, but to summarize, in a very rudimentary way, what I had never known, and what most of my friends have forgotten. Anyone who wants a more detailed and profound discussion of Christianity must turn to books by veteran Christians.

One word in conclusion. If the reader detects echoes of *The Book of Common Prayer* in a few places, that is because I happen to belong to the Episcopal Church. Nothing is farther from my thoughts at this moment than to be the special pleader for any one communion of Christians. Before deciding where the central truths of Christianity are best preserved, we must decide whether Christianity has any truths worth preserving.

Several of the editors of Harper and Brothers, together with a number of theologians representing various Christian traditions, read this book in manuscript form, and by their comments and criticisms greatly aided me in the task of preparing the final version. Three of my personal friends—Miss Viola C. White, and Professor and Mrs. Robert O. Fink—also read the manuscript, and offered suggestions of very real value.

Most of all I am indebted to my wife, Eva, who has helped me at every stage of my work. More times than I could mention she has spotted fallacies in reasoning or passages where the emphasis in thought was misplaced. It is a cliché to say that she has been my severest critic, but the statement is true. More to the point, she has also been my most helpful critic.

CHAD WALSH

Beloit College
October, 1946

Stop Looking and Listen

Chapter 1. SECULAR OPTIMISM
AND THE SADNESS OF
OUR TIMES

>>>>>>>>>>>>>>>>>>>>>>> <<<<<<<<<<<<<<<<<<<<<<<

The separation of Church and State is a fundamental principle
of American government. No bishops or presbyters sit in the
Senate by virtue of their ecclesiastical position. There is no
Church of America. Methodists, Roman Catholics, Christian
Scientists, Episcopalians, Baptists, and Unitarians all erect
churches and compete on equal terms for members. No denomination receives special favors from official quarters.
Protestant ministers, Roman Catholic priests, and Jewish rabbis are impartially summoned to pray for Congress.

America has no established religion, but it does have a
popular philosophy or attitude-toward-life which numbers
among its adherents a majority of the population. The living
faith of the people is not to be ascertained by reading the Bible
or flipping through the Constitution and statute books. To
learn what we believe, one need only examine the popular
magazines, turn on the radio, go to the movies, or listen to
any casual conversation in any corner drugstore.

The philosophy revealed by such down-to-earth sources is
one which inspires a quasi-religious spirit of devotion and self-

sacrifice on the part of its followers. Far more than Christianity or any other traditional religion, it shapes the day-by-day lives of the man in the street, the man in the swivel chair, and the man on the lecture platform. For lack of any better term, I shall use the colorless phrase, "Secular Optimism," to describe this national faith.

By Secular Optimism I mean a way of looking at life which invariably involves an implicit, almost mystical trust in the Scientific Method and in Automatic Moral Progress. In the simpler and more prevalent forms of Secular Optimism, the following articles of faith are prominent:

The universe is a huge machine, composed of matter and energy, or of something which is sometimes matter and at other times energy—a basic matter-energy or energy-matter. How the universe came into being is a useless speculation; probably it has always existed. Simple forms of life somehow evolved from matter in the remote past, and, by a gradual process of evolution, developed into more complicated types. The struggle for survival put a premium on intelligence, and pushed man along toward his dominant position in the world. Human history is the record of man's slow but steady advance toward control of his environment. All the apparent mysteries of the universe and human nature will gradually fade away as science extends the scope of its researches. In time we shall understand everything. Meanwhile, science is developing the techniques which will usher in Utopia in the not too distant future. Utopia will consist of plenty to eat for everyone, friendly relations among men, and abundant leisure for the cultivation of hobbies and the arts. The cruelty and stupidity which have always marked human life are easily explained by the fact that man has only recently emerged from brutishness, and is still addicted to "cultural lag"—a stubborn insistence on clinging to outmoded customs and habits of thought. These regrettable features of the human scene will soon be eliminated, as men learn to live by reason and utilize the resources of science. Man is by nature good and is getting better all the time.

The metaphysical assumptions of Secular Optimism are generally agnostic, in so far as the disciples of the faith trouble themselves with metaphysics at all. Sometimes a faint flavor of Christianity is retained, by using the language of Christianity in a poetic way to express the flaming certainties of the newer faith. The more sophisticated Secular Optimists are inclined to introduce a shadowy deity called the Life-Force. But regardless of any talk of God or the Life-Force, Secular Optimism remains essentially secular: the deity, if he exists, occupies a small and inconspicuous corner of the canvas, and man stands in the center, busily pulling himself up by his bootstraps.

The interesting thing about this modern faith is that it has been the dominant philosophy of the American people for less than a century, and already it is showing signs of extreme old age. The man in the street may retain his devout trust in it, but the intellectuals—who are the man in the street fifty years ahead of the times—are in a fog of uncertainty. The apostles of Secular Optimism are mostly old men. John Dewey is fighting a forlorn rearguard action to preserve the faith intact, and H. G. Wells, in the last few months of his life, had come to despair of humanity.

Obviously, the falsity of a philosophy or religion cannot be measured by the lack of tranquil assurance on the part of its believers. If that were the case, the present state of Christianity would prove that it, too, is false. But it is worth noticing that the buoyant confidence of Christianity lasted for more than fifteen hundred years, and the certainties of Secular Optimism less than a century. The latter has still to beat down the last ramparts of the older faith, yet many of the men who were its high priests a decade ago talk and write in a vein which is hauntingly reminiscent of Matthew Arnold's lament:

> The Sea of Faith
> Was once, too, at the full, and round earth's shore
> Lay like the folds of a bright girdle furled.
> But now I only hear

> Its melancholy, long, withdrawing roar,
> Retreating, to the breath
> Of the night-wind, down the vast edges drear
> And naked shingles of the world.

Why this sadness of the modern age? I suggest that the answer is very simple: the facts of history refuse to tally with the basic assumptions of Secular Optimism.

If man is getting better and better, he has chosen peculiar ways to demonstrate it. If his misdeeds are to be explained by "cultural lag," it is curious that a country famous for its science and education should have slid back the most markedly. "Cultural lag" is too mild a term for what happened in Germany. Nothing in the medieval or ancient history of the Germans gave them a model for their recent mass production of murder and torture. It is hard to believe in the natural goodness of man when one talks to a survivor of Dachau. It is also hard to believe in inevitable progress when one wanders through what were once the great cities of Europe and Asia.

Meanwhile, a considerable number of people have come to recognize what only a few lone-wolf thinkers ventured to say in the nineteenth century: that science is morally neutral. It is a blessing or a curse, depending on the way it is used. Scientific medicine saves many lives, but in a future war it will have to race hard to keep up with the atomic bomb and its radioactive consequences. The very knowledge of germs which makes possible many of the miracles of medicine is being eagerly acquired by military specialists for the dissemination of epidemics when and if the national interests demand it. The pretty picture of science ushering in Utopia is now neatly balanced by another picture: science destroying most of the cities of the earth, and ushering their survivors into a new Stone Age.

Secular Optimism, having promised an earthly paradise, cannot say that all will be evened up in a future, transter-restrial life. It must bring in a brick-and-plastic Utopia on the continents of the familiar world. If it cannot meet the demands of its devotees—if, indeed, we seem farther from Utopia than fifty years ago—the converts will begin slipping away, and the inspirational rallies will take on an increasingly elegiac tone.

That is just what is happening. The most advanced thinkers are leaving the ship at a great rate. But they are swimming in different directions.

One sizable group of thinkers believes that "cultural lag" is holding us back like flypaper. We are too wishy-washy. A few strong shoves are needed to bring in Utopia. Eggs must be broken to make the omelette, but once it is made it will stay made. These impatient souls are the collectivists and statists of various kinds. The Communists are the most conspicuous and best organized. Nevertheless, they are probably less firmly entrenched among the vanguard of the thinkers than during the glorious days of the Popular Front in the thirties. It is the long-range misfortune of Communism that it is associated with one particular country. And the news is getting around that the Russians are human. They are almost like the men on Main Street. Important Communist bureaucrats are as eager to make a privileged niche for their sons as American businessmen are to worm their offspring into vice-presidencies of promising concerns. A new aristocracy has developed, and the "democracy" of Russia begins to bear a disquieting resemblance to that of the more benevolent monarchies of times gone by. The glowing prophecy of the withering away of the state has been filed in the archives of the NKVD.

These considerations do not trouble the more mystical Communists, but they do dampen the enthusiasm of potential converts. A straw in the wind is the reluctance of Socialists here, in England, and in western Europe to form a united front with the Communists. The idea is coming into many men's minds that full employment in a police state is not an adequate reward for being forbidden to write letters to the editor and make speeches in Hyde Park.

Historians of the future, I suspect, will look back with scholarly amusement on both the Communists and the Secular Optimists. For all their mutual scorn and distrust, they have more in common than they realize. Both camps believe in Salvation by History, Salvation by Science, and in a Utopia so alluring that St. John's Heaven seems a cheap Hollywood set. Where they differ is in the *means* of achieving Progress. Secular Optimists, being gentle folk, would like to drift along on the good will and common sense of mankind, and edge up to Utopia without any unpleasant incidents. The Communists want to drag Progress along by the hair and get the business over with. Communism is Secular Optimism carried to its logical conclusions and freed of inhibitions. The two faiths are equally shallow. Both are completely this-worldly; both profess to know everything about human nature when actually they know almost nothing.

Chaplains and other wishful thinkers have recently said many encouraging things about the soldier in the foxhole and his "return to religion." One may suspect, without undue cynicism, that most of the religious feeling generated by fear of death will fade as quickly as the other passions of war once normalcy returns. Most of the foxhole Christians will be content just to watch the Fords go whizzing by.

Of more future significance are a handful of lonely thinkers, who have come to realize that the ultimate questions of human life are religious ones. Such mystics as Aldous Huxley and Christopher Isherwood and such Christians as T. S. Eliot and W. H. Auden are two or three generations ahead of the times. They may be destined to exert a profound influence eventually, but for the time being their value lies in their uncompromising refusal to accept the ready-made answers of the day.

Meanwhile, the man in the street, though still loyal to the formal tenets of Secular Optimism, is vaguely troubled. The earthly paradise seems no nearer than it did in the golden age of Queen Victoria. It does not appear likely that our grand-children will move into the New Jerusalem.

As the hope of an early paradise fades, certain questions that we pushed aside in an earlier flush of enthusiasm have a fighting chance of invading our minds. Suppose we do get our Utopia? Suppose everyone has plenty of bread, beef, and caviar? Then suppose we discover that immortality is not a wistful dream but an inescapable fact? A full belly may be an inadequate preparation for everlasting life. It may be that we are not permitted to live like happy and virtuous animals, even though we are convinced that such an existence is our proper destiny.

We may, after all, succeed in building our Utopias, and we may even flit to other planets when our own grows too cold for life, but there is an excellent chance that a time will come when all heat is dispersed throughout the universe and ab-solute zero is the only weather report. Who then will write the definitive history of our triumphs?

The more thoughtful part of the population shows today the familiar symptoms of a severe hang-over. The long illusion is ending, but few can say what shall replace our discredited beliefs. It is a good time for considering the alternatives, and considering them with fresh minds. Out of confusion comes humility, and out of humility comes truth.

Chapter 2. THE STANDARD
STUMBLING BLOCKS

≫≫≫≫≫≫≫≫≫≫≫≫≫≫≫≫≫≫≪≪≪≪≪≪≪≪≪≪≪≪≪≪≪≪≪≪

The usual explanation of the decline of Christianity is: Science did it. Before Charles Darwin journeyed to South America and Thomas Henry Huxley brandished a piece of chalk, everyone went to church on Sunday and believed that God created the world on a certain day in 4004 B.C., fashioned Adam out of the handiest raw materials, and subsequently carved Eve out of his rib. After the dawn of science, the museums and test tubes of the modern world revealed the complete absurdity of religion.

No myth of modern times is more devoutly believed than this one, but it is nonetheless a myth. It puts the cart before the horse.

The truth is that science discredited nothing except that degenerate variety of Christianity which regarded the Bible as a laboratory manual, and thumbed through Genesis and Revelation to ascertain the mundane timetable, much as medieval soothsayers searched the hexameters of Virgil for the shape of things to come. The early Christians, who presumably knew as much about Christianity as the Fundamentalists of the nineteenth and twentieth centuries, did not worry over the date of Creation: the overwhelming fact was that God did the creating. The shape of the earth was a side issue to them; much more important was the certainty that God was present with them no matter where they traveled on the earth. The Apostles' Creed, which probably existed in an early form by the beginning of the second century, says nothing about believing the Bible from cover to cover, and indulges in no astronomical speculations beyond the bald statement: "I believe in God the Father Almighty, Maker of heaven and earth."

The rest of Christianity—all that matters in Christianity—has not been touched by science. Science describes how the universe has developed and behaved since it came into being: it has nothing to say about *how* it came into being. It classifies the things that can be put into a test tube or otherwise subjected to measurement and analysis: of necessity, it has nothing whatever to say about things that cannot be examined by its methods. If any scientist or camp follower of science says that nothing exists except the things that can be observed scientifically, he is speaking not as a scientist, but as an exceedingly opinionated philosopher. He may or may not be right. He may easily be as wrong as the layman who denies the existence of infrared rays because his eyes cannot see them, and he has not mastered extravisual methods of discerning them.

Science can say nothing for or against the existence of God, for there is no scientific technique for determining His existence. (For that matter, science can say nothing for or against the existence of fairies and elves, and for exactly the same reason.) Science also has nothing to say about the Christian doctrine of the Incarnation: the belief that at one particular time and place God became man. The reason science can say nothing is that scientific theories are based on repeated observations: the chemist knows that hydrogen and oxygen will combine to produce water, because he can make them do it as often as he pleases. Christianity says that God became man, but only once. There were no scientists present, and the experiment cannot be repeated in a laboratory. Finally, the miracles, which are often held up as impossible violations of natural law, are violations only if one believes that a few thousand years of haphazard observation and a few centuries of intensive observation of natural laws have been sufficient to discover the ultimate, rather than the proximate, laws—as though a race of short-lived midges, breeding dozens of generations in one summer, were to assume that trees always have leaves and that leaves are always green.

However, the important thing, psychologically speaking, is not that science does not impinge on Christianity, but that many people have found it convenient to believe that it did. Modern science has been developing at a time when man has been yearning for some good reason to cast off the inhibitions of religion and go all out at the business of setting himself up as a god in his own right. This human desire to be a god is nothing new; the oldest legends are full of it, and it provides the raw material of most history. The only difference is that in the last century or two man got his hands on techniques that seemed to give him a fair chance of success. Religion then became an influence that distracted him from the pursuit of self-deification. Though we cannot blame the scientists for it, modern science furnished us a "rationalization" (as the psychologist puts it) for pursuing ends which we wished ardently to pursue—ends about which science quite literally had nothing to say.

So far I have been speaking of the physical and biological sciences. The social sciences present a more complicated picture.

The typical social scientist starts out with the assumption that everything evolves from something. Just as a one-celled form of life becomes a two-celled form, so a particular culture evolves into another type. Stone ages lead to bronze ages, and bronze ages to iron ages. One thing produces another. Nothing ever comes in from the outside.

Religion, as seen by the social scientist, begins as crude animism. Every stone and tree has its spirit, and there are more gods than men to worship them. Gradually the idea develops that one god is more powerful than the rest, and one's primary loyalty should go to him. In the final stage, the lesser gods are eliminated altogether, and only God is left.

The Christian objects to nothing in this outline, but he and the social scientist draw opposite conclusions. The latter says, "See, religion has evolved like everything else. There's nothing final about it. It's as human as our banking system, and some day—like our banking system—may evolve itself away altogether." The Christian says, "Curious, isn't it, that religion seems most often to evolve in one direction? It's as though some inherent necessity keeps pulling it that way."

Anthropology and history now join hands and furnish the skeptic with detailed information on the various religions and their resemblances to Christianity. He learns that rites similar to baptism are found all over the world, and were common in the Roman Empire when Christianity began. He hears of the ancient mystery cults, their worship of slain gods, and their eucharistic meals. He discovers that late Greek philosophy had developed a concept of the "Word of God" (the *Logos*) which appears with few changes in the prologue to the Gospel According to St. John. What is Christianity then—a hodgepodge of the religions current in the first century A.D.?

There are two ways of looking at the relation between Christianity and the other religions flourishing about the time of Christ. One is to say that since the resemblances are so startling, Christianity must have been a successful snowball that picked up all the loose objects in its path. Some germ of originality may be granted to it—a Jew by the name of Jesus really lived— but no one can say what the core is—the incrustations are too thick.

The other viewpoint is to say that no religion can be completely false, for every religion, even the queerest, is a reaching out after truth. If the worshipers of the imported gods of Egypt and the Near East addressed their deities as Saviour, it must have been because they felt that they needed a Saviour; if they practiced a rite like baptism, it was because they knew they needed to be purified and reborn; if they symbolically ate the flesh and drank the blood of their gods, it was because one needs to eat the flesh and drink the blood of God. In other words, truth floats around in a fragmentary state in the air, and groping men perceive it, even though they distort it and only half understand it. To the Christian the importance of Christ is not that He brought radically new ideas into the world, but that He confirmed the wistful old myths and day-dreams, and made them as real as bread and meat.

Actually, I am tilting a lance at straw men. We generally arrive at our beliefs not by a solemn process of laying all the cards on the table and comparing the suits, but by unconsciously drawing conclusions from our unspoken assumptions.

The unspoken assumptions are the things that nobody (or nobody who matters) would think of arguing about. One never sees two men, unless they are color blind, quarreling over whether green is green or red is red. They take it for granted. When a traffic light is to be erected, the difference between green and red is not debated. And when anyone tosses a ball into the air he never wonders whether it will come back to earth. The result is that he never thinks about gravitation at all, unless he is a scientist or philosopher.

In addition to assumptions of this sort, which are based on the objective facts of nature, there are the unspoken assumptions which are part of the "intellectual climate" of a given period, but are held as firmly as if they belonged in the law-of-gravitation class. Take the idea, "The new is always better than the old." It dominates the popular mind, and more often than not the learned mind as well.

The idea is utterly fantastic, of course, and breaks down in everyone's life at one time or another. The professional violinist does not look for the newest violin: he mortgages his future to buy a Stradivarius. The German democrats who opposed Hitler were not benighted old fogies for standing up against a tyranny which was literally something new under the sun.

Sometimes the new is better, sometimes the old. The man who looks for the best of everything will turn to ancient Greece for sculpture and to modern America for transportation.

One of the greatest psychological obstacles to the acceptance of Christianity is this worship of the new. "We live in a modern world; we have radios and electric refrigerators; our philosophy or religion must be modern, too. Christianity, that's old stuff." So something new is tried—such as philosophic materialism (which, as a matter of fact, is anything but new; it was clearly formulated by the Roman philosopher-poet, Lucretius, shortly before the time of Christ).

This awe in the presence of newness is closely related to the idea of evolution, which is the dominant concept of our age. The newest thing is good, because it represents the latest stage in evolution. (This belief, incidentally, is a perversion of Darwinism. "The survival of the fittest" concerns adaptation to environment, and has nothing to do with moral progress or any other kind of "progress.") The result of seeing evolution at work everywhere is to make incomprehensible another concept—one which is part of the bone and blood of Christianity: Revelation.

In modern thought, life is a closed circle. Once in the distant past something happened to bring life into being, but that is so far away it does not matter. After life began, it developed in complexity and variety within the tight little circle. One thing always led to another. If all the data could be collected, every development would be seen to be the result of previous causes.

Christianity does not deny that one thing leads to another, but it pictures another kind of life breaking into the closed circle. That kind of life touched the Hebrew prophets. Very likely it touched the Greek philosophers, too, and the originators of the mystery cults, and—for all we dare say to the contrary—the medicine men of Africa. Supremely and in an ultimate way it broke into the closed circle when Christ was born. Christ could never have been evolved. He could only be revealed.

Imagine a primitive Indian tribe living in the heart of Brazil. Its members are familiar with the country around them for thirty miles or so; beyond that, the world is a shadowland of fantastic beings and lurking enemies. Rumors have reached them once or twice of a body of water so wide that no one can see across it, but none of their members takes much stock in such tall talk. Now imagine that an explorer from the outside world comes into their closed circle. He tells them that indeed there is a great body of water—greater than he can express by any local comparisons. He speaks of the Atlantic Ocean and the Pacific Ocean, and tries to make them comprehend the singular fact that though there are two names it is really one body of water.

The explorer finally leaves, and returns to the outer world. After the men who have known him personally are all dead, some of the tribesmen will believe the legends of the great body of water that is called both the Atlantic Ocean and the Pacific Ocean, while others, with more "common sense," will point out that no one has ever seen this vast expanse of water, and the earth is not big enough to hold an ocean (or oceans) wider than the territory explored by the most courageous traveler of the tribe. A few of the tribesmen who believe in the two oceans may set out to find them, but the distances are so great that most of the adventurers will give up and return to face the ridicule of their neighbors. The very few that persevere are likely to spend a whole lifetime in reaching the coast, and by then they will be too feeble to work their way back through the jungle. However—and this is important—everyone, whether he believes in the tale of the original explorer or not—is affected by the fact that the explorer *was* real and did visit the tribe for a time. Much more is learned about the adjacent tribes, because the believers have to cross their lands on the exploring expeditions, and this knowledge is passed along to the whole tribe and has an effect on its diplomatic relations with neighboring groups. Less pleasant results also come about: friends argue and quarrel over the historicity of the explorer, and promising business partnerships and marriages break up when one party decides to undertake the great quest, and the other refuses to accompany him.

A limping analogy, admittedly. But Christianity says that something of this sort once happened. We try to live in a closed circle, where we know all the answers, but God won't let us alone. He breaks into the circle, and what He does becomes a *cause*.

Still another unspoken assumption is the idea that the importance of anything depends on size. The Empire State Building is more significant than the Parthenon to the average man, and *Gone with the Wind* is more memorable than *Ethan Frome*. The cruder forms of the worship of size are avoided by the intellectuals, but they succumb when it is a question of astronomy. Almost all of us have an inferiority complex because of Space. We have learned how tiny the earth is in comparison with the sun, and how infinitesimal the sun is beside many other stars. We almost feel sorry for our poor old sun. And the greatest stars are grains of sand compared to the cold, empty stretches of space between them. Interstellar space is the nightmare of the age; we feel it pressing down on us with impersonal hostility, and we dwindle to the size of fruit flies. We are too microscopic for God to notice us, even if God exists.

Amateurs are always speculating on whether life exists on other planets; they would feel more at home in the universe if they knew that the earth was not the only speck of dust with crawling things on it. However, though some day we may exchange radar signals with the Martians, there will still be the vast bleak spaces between the stars and galaxies of stars.

One might well ask, why the tacit assumption that no life exists in interstellar space? It is certainly very provincial of us to think that our own frail kind of life, which freezes at the North Pole and roasts at the Equator, is the only sort possible. Utterly different, but not less rational or loving, beings may thickly populate all the space that seems so hideous to us. But assume that they do not—that space *is* empty. Then the greater the glory of the earth, and the more breath-taking the estate of man. No one in his right senses pities the man who is fortunate enough to have a broad lawn covered with perfectly useless grass. Man is set in the limitless garden of space.

Chapter 3. AN OUTLINE OF CHRISTIANITY

>>>>>>>>>>>>>>>>>>>>>>>><<<<<<<<<<<<<<<<<<<<<<<<

I almost omitted this chapter and the next two. "After all," I can hear the reader saying, "everyone knows what Christianity is. The important question is whether it makes sense."

I finally decided to set down the A B C's of Christianity only because I am quite sure that millions of Americans do *not* have the faintest conception of what Christianity is. I recall the weird jumble of ideas in my own mind until a few years ago. Someone could have drawn a quaint mural at the expense of my ignorance: a naked couple eating an apple while a snake looks on happily, a man herding a menagerie into a homemade boat, three men in bright clothes looking at a star through Christmas-card snow—that was about all I knew of Christianity.

Dense though my ignorance was, I cannot believe that it was unique. Second- and third-generation agnostics now form a large part of the population, and many nominal Christians have gained nothing from their Sunday schools except skill in cutting out pictures, and nothing from their church services except the conviction that the mark of a Christian is a well-rounded personality.

I shall, therefore, assume that the reader knows little or

nothing about Christianity. Certainly the experienced and thoughtful Christian can tranquilly skip these three chapters. They are for elementary students like myself. All I want to do in them is describe the beliefs that most Christians have held in common for nineteen centuries.

Members of specific churches will undoubtedly wish I had emphasized certain doctrines more or played down others. Each church has a set of beliefs that it peculiarly cherishes, while the church across the street stresses another set. But despite all the bitterness of sectarian argument, and all the excommunicating and heresy hunting that have enlivened the history of Christianity, there is a central core of beliefs—a sort of common denominator—which is very obvious to the outside observer.

The Christian first of all conceives of God, who has always been, and will always be. If the universe should utterly vanish, God would still be—forever. Expressions of time cannot be applied to God. He is timeless, the "Eternal Now." He lives not in time but in eternity. The human mind, chained as it is to clocks and calendars, cannot imagine eternity (children can come closer to it than adults), but Christianity makes the flat statement that God stands entirely outside of time, even the greatest reaches of time that we can picture in our minds. From the human viewpoint, He was, He is, He will be. From His own point of view, He *is*—eternally.

Strictly speaking, time did not exist until after the Creation of the universe. It is, therefore, absurd to speak of a "time before the Creation." There was no time, only eternity. But our minds being what they are, we may say that, from our viewpoint, God created or began to create the universe at a certain time in the very remote past. (We have no reason to assume that the process of Creation is over. God may still be making suns and planets; some day we may discover a new solar system in our section of the universe.)

God created the universe just as a sculptor creates a statue, except that the sculptor works with material which already exists—clay, marble, bronze—whereas God brought "matter-energy" into being by a sheer act of the will. This, again, is an idea that the human mind cannot conceive: when men create something, they use material already at hand. When God created the universe, it was as though a musician composed a melody in his mind and the music became so real to his inner ear that it burst the bounds of his mind and began sounding in the air.

At first glance it may seem of no importance whether God created the universe from scratch, or whether He found the materials already existing and set about imposing form and order upon them. The second idea is a common one in philosophy. However, if "matter-energy" existed independently of God, and God set about manipulating it the way a sculptor handles a block of marble from a quarry, it is very easy to assume that there is something recalcitrantly evil about the material world; that God must wrestle with it, and man had best bypass it and live as much like a disembodied spirit as possible. Christianity, like Judaism, asserts that the material world is good, because God created it and God is good.

But first—*is* God good? Perhaps He created the universe and its inhabitants solely for the pleasure of watching creatures suffer. The whole universe may be a huge concentration camp, and God the master sadist, pulling the strings on the puppets and laughing with delight when He observes their agonies. Perhaps Himmler was truly created in the image of his Maker. This idea of God cannot be tossed aside lightly. The dispassionate man from Mars, watching a cross section of humanity day by day, might conclude that misery far outweighs happiness; that the cards are stacked against us.

If God is the Super-Nazi, then nothing you or I can do will save us from His unwelcome attentions. He may tease us with false hopes, but the steel whips are hanging on the wall, and the crematorium is waiting for us when He has had His fun. The most we can do is curse the torturer, or else try to forget about Him, and eat, drink, and be merry as long as He will allow us to; then die with the hope (but without the assurance) that the crematorium is really the end—that He has no further torments for us.

But there is a second and more common way of looking at God. It is particularly fashionable today, though it is another of those "modern" ideas that are hoary with antiquity. Perhaps God is not interested in you and me at all. He may have performed the act of Creation in the spirit of a scientific experimenter, or perhaps He was like an artist, brimming with vitality, who dashes off a series of paintings, but loses interest in them once he sees them hanging on the museum wall. God gave life a start, and then left it alone. Wherever His attention may be directed now, it is not toward us.

This second God is also of no importance whatever to us, except as a philosophic notion. He will not aid us, reward us, nor punish us. Humanity is completely on its own, and God is completely on His own.

Christians believe in neither the Sadist God nor in an indifferent Deity. Theirs is a personal God with a personal interest in everything, great or small. He knows the number of hairs on your head, and the thoughts in your mind. He thinks in terms of right and wrong, uncompromisingly lines Himself up on the side of right, and insists that you and I take sides, too.

The existence of such a God as Christians worship is not at first self-evident. On the surface He is less plausible than the Sadist God or the impersonal First Cause. However, even without the aid of Revelation, it is possible for a shrewd observer of human affairs to come to a belief in Him. Indeed, it is hard not to, for human nature can be explained only on the assumption that God exists, and that He has the characteristics that Christians attribute to Him.

There are two types of people who are part of the stock in trade of any novelist. The first is the man who does much talking about morality but in practice is a shifty customer, nasty to his friends and less given to acts of kindness than many people who prate less about virtue.

Type two is less conspicuous, but can be found on any street. This is the man who believes devoutly that right is right and wrong is wrong and who tries to live a good life, but cannot make a go of it. He knows that he ought to be faithful to his wife, but he sneaks off with the first woman who smiles at him. He knows that he drinks too much, but he can never resist an invitation from the boys.

There is a third type which has been curiously neglected by those astute sociologists, the novelists. Perhaps he has existed on a large scale only in modern times, and no pigeonhole has as yet been assigned to him. I am thinking of the man who proudly proves to you that morality is relative—it all depends on the way you look at it, and where you grew up. His mind is an anthology of anecdotes about exotic tribes in which polygamy is the rule, other tribes where polyandry prevails; islands of remote seas in which cannibalism is as respectable as beef-eating, and other spots on the map where superannuated members of the clan are piously put to death. Armed with these facts, he assures you that a distaste for stealing or murder is purely a cultural prejudice.

Now the curious thing about type three is that more often than not, quite inconsistently with his expressed opinions about virtue, he will walk ten miles to pay back a dime, and is quick on the trigger in defense of any person who (to use old-fashioned language) has been "unjustly" treated.

When World War II arrived, many of my friends suffered from a split personality. Their efforts to divest themselves of cultural concepts of right and wrong were truly heroic. They trained themselves to pick up the afternoon paper and read about the massacre of the Jews in central Europe or the obliteration of a rebellious village and say philosophically, "It all depends on the way you look at it. According to Hitler's moral standards, he's doing the right thing." But if the same newspaper told of the forced evacuation of the Nisei from the West Coast, they would burst forth in fiery indignation and say that citizens of a country in which such vile deeds occurred were unworthy to drop blockbusters on Germany.

The psychologists have not yet explored the depths of this peculiarly modern type of split personality. When they get around to it, I suspect that they will find that the man who acts as though he believes in right and wrong, but will not own up to it, is as twisted up inside as the traditional hypocrite who talks like a Sunday-school teacher and lives like a confidence man.

It begins to look as if no one can get away from this idea of right and wrong, even if he rules it out of his list of approved concepts. It is as persistent as the sexual instinct or the hunger for food.

Nor does the theory that morality is purely a product of environment hold water. Admittedly the details vary from culture to culture, but there is still a suspicious similarity among all moral codes. Fair play and courage are generally admired; stabbing-in-the-back and cowardice are despised in almost every community from London to Timbuktu. Solicitude for one's parents is well-nigh universally commended, even though (as in the case of some tribes in rigorous climates) it may involve euthanasia for the old and feeble.

Morality is not mere conformity to local likes and dislikes. Often the moral sense drives a man to outraging public opinion: the gallows or the stake has frequently been the reward of the moral man. It won't do to say, either, that morality is *merely* a set of habits sanctioned by society for its own survival. The impulse that makes a poor swimmer jump into the river to rescue someone, when he knows he is almost certain to drown in the attempt, injures society by depriving it of two lives instead of one. There is another difference between this persistent idea of right and wrong, and social customs that are often the outgrowth of a particular culture. An American who has been accustomed to drive on the right-hand side of the road can go to England and keep to the left. A Pole, who presumably has been conditioned from childhood to regard autocratic government as normal, can come to America and learn democratic ways. But the stubborn idea that there is such a thing as right and that it is different from another thing called wrong seems impossible to shake off. It is more like the color of your eyes or the shape of your skull.

Environment won't explain it all. The only other explanation available is this: right and wrong correspond to something outside of man. That something is not always perceived with perfect accuracy. It is like the value of π. Some people come closer to it than others. Some say 3, some 3 1/7, some 3.1416, and only a handful, perhaps, know the answer to the twentieth decimal. But, more or less exactly, every human being in the world is conscious of this something which beats at his perceptions—even though he may choose to go counter to the knowledge it imparts.

Let us see what point we have reached. Christianity says that God has always been. He is the Creator of the material universe and of life. (From our human viewpoint, we can say that God caused life to evolve from single cells to its present complexity. From God's vantage point of eternity, the stages of "evolution" are a series of events, occurring simultaneously; we perceive them only as they are translated into time.) God, however, is not only the Creator. He is intensely concerned with right and wrong, and insists that men share His concern.

Now we come to another problem. If God is the Source of our ideas of right and wrong, why don't we live up to God's standards of right? Why is the world filled with hypocrites who preach one thing and practice another, and why do all of us so often find it impossible to do the thing we ought to do or avoid the thing we know we ought to avoid?

What Christianity says is this: When man was first created (or, if you prefer, when the anthropoids definitely evolved into man) he existed in a state of natural harmony with God. He did the right thing and avoided the wrong thing, because anyone in complete harmony with God will conform to God's will. This was not the slavish obedience that a human despot demands of his subjects. God did not desire man's obedience for the sense of power it gave Him: He was already all-powerful. He desired man's obedience because that is the natural relation between the Creator and the beings He has brought into existence, and the only relation that permits them *to be themselves*. By virtue of his obedience, man enjoyed true liberty. He could innocently do anything he wanted to, for he wanted to do only what was right. Compared with this early freedom, our modern civic liberties are a sad patchwork of compromises, for mankind, in its present state, can never think of liberty without surrounding it with safeguards to protect individuals from its abuse. Our laws against robbery and murder are a real limitation on our liberty, for we frequently want to steal and kill. Paradisaical man knew no such restraints. He could steal and kill all he wanted to, because he never wanted to.

This picture of original goodness runs counter to the popular thinking of the day. We like to flatter ourselves by picturing our remote ancestors as hairy roughnecks. We expect mankind to be perfect in the future, not in the past. "Doesn't everyone know that man started out as a brute, scarcely distinguishable from the apes, and only evolved a sense of right and wrong after millenniums of trial and error?" is the usual question.

This whole matter has been treated in brilliant detail by C. S. Lewis in his book, *The Problem of Pain*.[1] I shall pause here only to point out what seem to me two fallacies in the popular viewpoint. The argument assumes, first of all, that man has been becoming better and better. There is no shred of proof for this. The men of ancient Rome and the Middle Ages may have enslaved the peoples they conquered, but it was left for modern man to invent biological warfare, such as the Germans waged against the Jews and Poles. To find a people whose

[1] New York: The Macmillan Company, 1945. See especially chap. IV, "Human Wickedness."

delight in torture and murder rivaled that of the Nazis one would need to turn to the ancient Assyrians.

In the second place, if the Christian account of man's history is true, we cannot judge early men by ourselves, nor by the most primitive tribes in out-of-the-way places. The artifacts of early man may have been crude, and he may have been hairy and coarse-skinned, but his moral nature is forever a closed book to science. Something happened to mark a sharp break in the history of man, and we who are on one side of that chasm can never determine by sheer reason or investigation what life was like on the other side.

We come, therefore, to one of the most unpopular doctrines of Christianity: the Fall and Original Sin.

The mention of the Fall calls up in most people's minds the familiar picture of an apple tree, a serpent, and a naked couple. It is almost as hard to talk seriously about the Fall as it would be to use *Sleeping Beauty* as the basic text of a course in philosophy.

Let us first get rid of the idea that a fruit tree necessarily had anything to do with the Fall of man. It may very well have been the immediate occasion of the Fall, of course. When a man turns robber, he can as easily start out by stealing apples as foreign markets, and when paradisaical man turned rebel against God he may have rebelled in a way that, *on the surface,* seems too trivial to have momentous consequences. But the chance opportunity of the rebellion does not matter. In one way or another, man tried to set himself up on his own. He chose to smash the natural harmony that made obedience to God a joyous thing. And he succeeded.

Why did he succeed? God gave man free will. If anyone thinks that foolish or unkind of God, let him ask himself, "Would I like my children to live in a world in which they were *forced* to be good?" The most benevolent of tyrants turn men into automatons. If man does not have the freedom to do wrong, there is no significance in doing right. God apparently thought the risk was worth the price—that only by giving man freedom of choice could he implant any meaning in his life. We may reproach God with giving us too much rope, but if we do that we must abandon the other charge often leveled against Him: that He is an arbitrary tyrant.

In any case, early man took advantage of his free will and chose to go his own way, and this desire is a part of every one of us today. Why did he do this? What could have put the idea into his head, if he was already in such a state of harmony with God that doing the right thing was as natural to him as it is difficult to us? The answer of Christianity is: the Devil.

By the Devil I do not mean a symbol of evil, nor a symbol of imperfection, nor a symbol of cultural lag. I do not mean a symbol of anything. The Devil is not a poetic concept nor a figure of speech. According to the Christian tradition, the Devil was once an angel, but he rebelled against God, and then set about winning mankind over to his side. In other words, the Fall of man was antedated by the Fall of Lucifer.

This, of course, only pushes the mystery farther back. Why did Lucifer the angel rebel against God? Nobody knows, nor apparently can know, the ultimate origin of evil. Neither Christianity nor any other religion has any explanation of its existence; neither does any philosophical system; and, of course, science has not one word to say about it. Evil just *is*. All we can know about it is that if a being—whether angel or human —has free will there is always the possibility that he may choose to misuse it: that he will conceive of some lesser ideal and abandon the greater one. Whatever the reason, Lucifer became the Devil, and went about the task of propagandizing mankind with phenomenal success. He has been our constant companion to this very day.

This brings up another question. When Lucifer turned bad, why did not God destroy him, and save mankind from being tempted? No one should presume to give a pat answer to this. Trying to read God's mind is more difficult—and more presumptuous—than psychoanalyzing paradisaical man. But, to put it in earthly terms, it seems likely that God believed the issue might as well be faced one time as another. Man would choose either to maintain the divine harmony in which he lived, or to turn away from it. If the Devil were destroyed, some new tempter would come along. If God forestalled every menace to man's virtue, what would become of free will? Man would have been like the pupils in some "progressive" schools who are protected against such harsh realities as grades and compulsory assignments, but who are subtly manipulated into doing what the teacher thinks they ought to do. Some day— sooner or later—man had to take his stand. He took it.

The harmony between man and God, the joy of obedience to God, the perfect liberty of submission to God, came to an end. From the wreckage two things survived: a vague sense of right and wrong (which was as often violated as obeyed) and the almost universal legend of a golden age in the distant past. But the golden age was over, and the stage was set for the misery, confusion, and despair of the greater part of recorded history. Not until a little over nineteen hundred years ago did anything happen to mark another break in human history as definite and final as man's Fall from blessedness.

Chapter 4. AN OUTLINE OF CHRISTIANITY, *Continued*

>>>>>>>>>>>>>>>>>>>>>>>>>>><<<<<<<<<<<<<<<<<<<<<<<<<<<

More than three thousand years ago a wandering tribe of Semites began drifting and fighting their way into a small tract of land that bordered on the eastern Mediterranean. They worshiped a god of storm and fire named Yahweh, who had his headquarters on a mountain called Sinai in the Arabian Desert, and they were sure he championed them against the gods of the older inhabitants of the territory. Frequently they deserted him for the neighboring gods, but always they returned to him, and century by century their understanding of his nature altered.

With the advent of the later prophets from about the sixth century B.C. on, Yahweh had come to be regarded not as a local or tribal deity but as the only God there is—the Creator of the universe, the God whose will in the end controls every nation and every member of every nation. This idea became so firmly implanted in the minds of the Jews that neither the Assyrian kings nor the Macedonian despots nor the Roman emperors could wipe it out by slavery or blood.

But the Jews did more than become monotheists. They united belief in God with morality. God to them was not a mere Creator, indifferent to the deeds of the market place, and

Himself free to live the life of a sultan in a harem. Nor was morality a prudent set of precepts, sanctioned by the common sense of the race *and nothing more*. Yahweh was Himself completely just and He demanded justice from those who would be His. He was the sanction of morality.

Add to these two developments in knowledge of the divine nature the further realization of other prophets that the Almighty is also a God of love, ready to forgive the penitent sinner, and there was ample reason for the Jews to be regarded as a peculiar people. While the Greek poets were retelling the lovely and racy stories of the private lives of the divinities, and the Greek philosophers were intellectually analyzing the bases of the moral life, the Jews were passionately seeing the hand and will of a just and compassionate God in every choice they had to make in their day-by-day lives. The Greeks compartmentalized their lives; religion and morality with them had little or nothing to do with each other. Jewish life knew no compartments, for God was all in all.

No wonder, then, that the Jews considered themselves a people apart. Other nations shared their opinion. And no wonder that the Jews developed a combination of national and religious cohesiveness that has preserved them as a distinct group to this day. Their sense of apartness was created at a time when the rest of the Mediterranean world was living in a fantasy of childish religion, and morality was the concern of the academies.

The Jews had the Ten Commandments and they also had the great mass of Mosaic tradition—customs at first passed down orally by the rabbis and then written down—a body of material eventually regarded as equally binding with the Ten Commandments. The way to live was as definitely outlined as a chemistry experiment. The answers were all there. But gradually something happened. It may have been partly the misery of being ruled by foreigners. More likely it was a realization of having reached a dead end. The Jews knew, in minute detail, what to do in any given situation, but very often they did something else. Like men in all periods of history, they showed a perverse inclination to preach one thing and practice another. More and more, morality became bogged down in red tape. Ritual and customs grew more and more complicated. A complete observance of all the religious commandments and taboos demanded an independent income, because so many practical inconveniences were entailed. The men who succeeded in living up to every subclause of the moral code were often well aware of their virtue, and expected to be admired by less virtuous neighbors. Somehow the crop of saints produced by the Law was disappointingly small.

The experience of the Jewish people had proved: (1) Anyone can have a detailed knowledge of right and wrong and yet fail to live by it; (2) men who completely live up to the code of morality are frequently harsh and unloving toward their fellows; (3) serving God and trying to obey His laws is not a guarantee of earthly prosperity—the legions of Rome controlled Palestine as completely as they did Gaul, though the fiction of self-government was maintained. The thin pretense of autonomy was possible only as long as the high priesthood and other ruling groups played the part of quislings.

Was this the culmination of the vision that had set the Jews apart? A nation uneasily co-operating with the colossus of the Mediterranean, and a society shot through with misery, hypocrisy, injustice, and an intolerable sense of guilt.

Little by little a mood developed. Something had to happen to break into the circle. Only intervention by God could wipe the slate clean and leave it ready for a living message. Only a messiah could save the people from themselves.

This idea of a messiah is well-nigh impossible to analyze in the cold language of historical research. The Jews themselves were not sure what he would be. Some saw him in crude political terms—the super-leader who would expel the Romans and bring the whole world under the benevolent rule of the Jews. Others thought of him more as one who would make real the relationship between God and man that hovered as a haunting possibility on the fringes of consciousness. It does not greatly matter what the Jews expected of the messiah. When a man is hungry, he may dream of bread, steak, or oyster stew, but in any case he knows that he needs food.

Let us leave the Jews now and turn to the Greeks. As much as a century before the time of Socrates there existed a sharp cleavage between the traditional religion and the morality of the learned. Philosophers might still speak vaguely of Zeus and Apollo and perform the ancient rites, but their ethical thinking was on a much more abstract plane, where the love life of the gods and goddesses had little place. Playwrights might still use the familiar deities as dramatis personae, but the old implicit faith began to fade into poetry among the high-brows and held its own only among simple and uneducated people, such as the peasants and fishermen.

Nothing could be more false than to imagine that Christianity burst into a Greek world where men were passionately devoted to Zeus and his underling gods. Jehovah and Zeus did not stage a knockdown battle for the worship of the Hellenes. Instead, Christianity came on the Greek scene when the Greeks were in a state of religious and intellectual confusion, doubt, and experimentation that makes one think of the varied cults and philosophies of southern California today.

The brilliant period of Socrates and Plato was followed by centuries of thought,[1] during which the concept of one God

---

[1] Anyone wishing a detailed treatment of late Greek philosophy and the mystery cults can profitably consult Professor Erwin R. Goodenough's *Religious Tradition and Myth* (New Haven: Yale University Press, 1937). My only quarrel with Professor Goodenough is that he seems to make a mistake typical of most social scientists. He assumes that because Christianity resembles a number of other religions and philosophies current around the time of Christ it must be a composite affair. I consider the opposite true. The other faiths were foreshadowings of Christianity. I am happy to find that Norman Powell Williams' accurate and penetrating article on the mystery cults in *Essays Catholic & Critical* (edited by Edward Gordon Selwyn [New York: The Macmillan Company, 1926]) bears me out in this opinion of the usual secularistic analysis.

increasingly predominated. This God is almost as hard to pin down as the Jewish messiah. He is best looked upon as the Ultimate Source. Sometimes He was compared to the sun, which seems to be giving forth light and heat eternally without any loss. One writer likened Him to a Persian king, who is never seen by his subjects, but whose commands are enforced by his agents everywhere in his territory. With this God of the later Greek philosophers we are very close to the God of Christianity—as some of the early Christian writers acknowledged —but to the end He remained a cold and abstract God—the sort of being that is intellectually plausible, but difficult to love and address in prayer. He was a high-brow God.

The masses of people, no longer satisfied by the old deities, began to turn to strange gods—mostly importations from Egypt and the Near East. By the time of Christ the priests of their mystery cults were doing a thriving business.

The mystery cults, too, are enveloped in a good deal of uncertainty when the modern historian confronts them. Their secrets were zealously guarded by the initiates, and Christianity, which fought a life-and-death battle with one of the cults (Mithraism) did not go out of its way to preserve data for the research scholars of the twentieth century. The little that has survived shows that a common pattern ran through many of them. There was the idea of the suffering god—the god who, under different names in the different cults, came down to earth and died in various fashions. His death worked a change in mankind's condition—a change for the better.

Anyone wishing to be initiated into one of the cults underwent an elaborate ritual of purification (involving, for instance, being drenched with the blood of a sacrificial animal). There was often a group meal, held at regular intervals, at which the initiates ate food symbolizing the slain god, and in this way established a closer relation to him.

The mystery cults lacked backbone. Their members drifted from one cult to another, as their modern equivalents do, or belonged to several cults simultaneously. The world of the mystery cults was a twilight one, lit up by the changing colors of the imagination. The more thoughtful worshipers knew that they were adoring poetic symbols rather than the ultimate reality. They often specified a dozen different mystery gods in one prayer, using the names as synonyms for the one God. But for all their vagueness, the mystery cults thrived because they fed the spiritual hunger of men who could no longer believe in the childish deities of the classical world, and who were left emotionally starved by the God of the philosophers. Such men found in a mystery cult a god whose suffering made him akin to them in their misery, and whose hands were always outstretched to meet their own imploring hands.

Such was the state of the Mediterranean world as the time of Christ's advent drew near. The Jews had their passionate monotheism, a divinely sanctioned moral code, and some glimpses into the mercy of their deity, but they were tormented by the gap between knowledge and practice. Sluggish peasants in out-of-the-way parts of the Greco-Roman world still worshiped the ancient gods, but the main tide of thought had swept past them. The philosophers had their sober concept of one God, but He was too much like one of Plato's "ideas" for the heart to beat wildly at mention of His name. And everywhere over the Mediterranean world the mystery cults swarmed in from exotic lands, to bring men a make-believe faith in a god nearer to man and more loving than any the dramatic poets or the philosophers had to offer.

The Mediterranean world was waiting. Men who sought ultimate meaning felt an incompleteness, a need for God's intervention. Something had to happen. What Christianity says is that something did happen, something in the light of which the different fragments of insight about the nature of God, the nature of things, and the nature of man, were all shown to be partially true. They fitted into The Truth.

Chapter 5. AN OUTLINE OF CHRISTIANITY, *Concluded*

>>>>>>>>>>>>>>>>>>>>>> <<<<<<<<<<<<<<<<<<<<<<<

Nearly two thousand years ago a Jew by the name of Jesus was born in the town of Bethlehem. We know almost nothing of the first thirty years of his life. The Four Gospels of the New Testament describe the last two or three years in some detail, though even for that period we have nothing approaching a day-by-day biography. We know that he wandered about Palestine, teaching by means of short anecdotes, and healing the sick, and that gradually a group of followers gathered around him and went with him on his travels. Finally, he was arrested and sentenced to death for what seem to have been reasons partly of a religious and partly of a political nature. He was executed one Friday by the standard Roman method of crucifixion. On the following Sunday his tomb was found empty, and he reappeared among his followers, stayed with them for several weeks, and then vanished from their sight.

Such is the bare outline of Christ's life. The non-Christian, naturally enough dismissing the Resurrection as a myth, is puzzled to know why this Jewish teacher of the first century should be accorded the honors due only to God. He may have lived a good life, and taught his disciples a lofty code of ethics, but the same could be said of Hosea or Socrates. There seems something strained, even idolatrous, in the Christian attitude toward this man who lived so long ago.

The position of Christianity is that the love, adoration, and obedience that are due only to God are given to Christ because He was—and is—God.[1] He was completely God, and at the same time completely man.

He was not God pretending to be man. The body that his followers saw was not an optical illusion created by God to keep them from being frightened. His physical body was like yours and mine. When He fasted, He grew hungry; when He walked a long distance He knew what it was to be tired and sleepy.

Christ was fully human, but also fully God. This does not mean that He was *simply* a very good man, though He was certainly that. It does not mean that He was *simply* the ideal

[1] The reader will observe that I am bypassing the Trinity. I do this merely because any adequate discussion of the doctrine would double the size of this book, and I do not feel that a treatment of it is essential for a very elementary work. I consider the doctrine profoundly true, and some understanding of it is essential for the devotional and intellectual life of any Christian who wants to progress beyond the kindergarten stage of religion. The important thing to remember about the Trinity is that the concept was not dreamed up by a group of theorists who had nothing better to do. Rather, it was an idea that the early Christians, almost against their wills, were compelled to work out, because otherwise their religious experience made no sense. The Jews who were Christ's first followers were familiar with God the Father—the Creator of the universe and the personal God of every man. The quality of Christ's life and His triumph over death convinced them that He, too, was God—yet while He was on earth with them they had heard Him pray to God the Father. After Christ was no longer visible to them, His disciples had the experience of Pentecost, when they suddenly acquired spiritual powers they had never dreamed of. These three experiences of the first Christians have been repeated by Christians ever since. They have perceived God as the Absolute, the Source, the Creator (God the Father). They have also perceived Him as they prayed to Christ or felt His presence in Holy Communion (God the Son). And they have felt God at work inside of them, giving them new strength and courage and understanding (God the Holy Ghost). Whatever the Trinity means, it does *not* mean that there are three Gods. Christianity is as fiercely monotheistic as Judaism or Mohammedanism.

man—the ultimate possibility of manhood—though He was that, too. He was God, the same God who created the universe, life, indeed the very flesh and bones that became His when He was born in Bethlehem.

Theologians are careful to say that God became "man," not "a man." The distinction may appear a trivial one at first sight, but is actually of vital importance. If, by the Incarnation, God had merely become *a* man, the event would have been an interesting historical freak, but nothing that could affect us for good or evil almost two millenniums later. But the traditional view of the Incarnation is quite different: when Jesus was born, God became incarnate in human nature—your nature, my nature, the nature of everyone and for all time. What Jesus did, and what He was, therefore affected and affects every human being in the world.

If God chose to become man, what was His reason? One reason we are sure of, but I shall defer discussion of it for the moment. There may have been additional or secondary reasons. One probable purpose, for example, was to show mankind what God is like. We can understand God only when He is translated into human terms. It is no accident that the God of so many religions is anthropomorphic—that He is a glorified man. God has to be put into terms that we can think about, and the highest we can think about is human.

Another purpose may well have been to confirm the moral teachings of the best thinkers and religious leaders before the time of Christ. I say *confirm,* for there is little or nothing new in what Christ taught about ethics. He did not introduce unheard-of ideas; instead, he confirmed beyond future argument the sense of right and wrong that people already had. Once they had wondered; now they knew.

The Mosaic Law had taught men to love God; the prophets had taught them to love one another. Christ did not invert nor modify the law of love. Instead, he restated it in the briefest and most memorable of words: "Thou shalt love the Lord thy God with all thy heart, and with all thy soul, and with all thy mind. This is the first and great commandment. And the second is like unto it; Thou shalt love thy neighbor as thyself. On these two commandments hang all the Law and the Prophets."

If God became man only or primarily to show mankind what God is like, to set a good example, and to teach the ultimate basis of morality, that day in Bethlehem was the darkest day of human history. Everyone's sins are ten times blacker than before, because Christ throws such a pitiless blaze of demand on human conduct. If that was all there was to the coming of Jesus, W. H. Auden was right to make Herod say in the Christmas oratorio, *For the Time Being,*[2]

And suppose, just for the sake of argument . . . that this child is in some inexplicable manner both God and man, that he grows up, lives, and dies, without committing a single sin? Would that make life any better? On the contrary it would make it far, far worse. For it could only mean this; that once having shown them how, God would expect every man, whatever his fortune, to lead a sinless life in the flesh and on earth. Then indeed would the human race be plunged into madness and despair.

Fortunately for our sanity, Christianity does not say that God became man primarily in order to simplify or amplify the Ten Commandments, or to show us a perfect being in action. He became man in order to die for man's redemption.

The doctrine of the Atonement shares with Original Sin and Hell the honor of being peculiarly offensive to the modern taste. But before dismissing it as a bloodthirsty relic of the savage past, it is well to ask ourselves: What were the alternatives that confronted God?

Remember that He was dealing with a race of beings who had turned from Him and grown hardened in their ways. Because they had turned from Him, no complete unity between Himself and them was possible. However kind and loving a

[2] New York: Random House Inc., 1944, p. 124. Quoted by courtesy of the publishers.

father may be, he can never be on terms of complete intimacy with his son if the latter insists on robbing banks and striking his old mother.

One obvious solution of the problem would have been for God to wipe the human race off the face of the planet. We cannot doubt that He had—and has—the power to do just this, but few of us, I imagine, will reproach Him for refraining from so drastic a settlement of the impasse.

Another alternative, as I have suggested earlier, was for God to act like a benevolent dictator. He could have compelled man—conditioned him from conception—to be good. The world would then have been filled with smiling faces, and everyone would have loved his neighbor as himself. Wars and petty spite would have faded into incomprehensible legends. Man would have been as uniformly virtuous as a lion is carnivorous. And, since virtue was compulsory, it would have meant nothing. If, as we may suspect, one reason God created man was to give meaning to goodness by making it optional, any program of obligatory goodness would have been to close down the laboratory and file away the experiment as a failure.

A third alternative was for God to smile and say boys will be boys. He could have left people alone, and forgiven them all they chose to do, and welcomed one and all into a cozy heaven. To do this would have been to act the part of the indulgent father who says, "Yes, my son robs banks and slaps his old mother black and blue, but I won't let that impair my relationship with him." But *could* God do this? He was the God of love, but He was also the Source and Sanction of morality, as well as being the Creator of those beings called men. Could He go against His own nature? Call it a limitation on God's power, if you will. The words are not worth quibbling about. I prefer to think that the very word *God* includes the idea of a stern insistence on the difference between right and wrong, and that if this insistence is wiped away, the word no longer means God.

The fourth alternative is the one God chose. He took our

sins upon Himself. The burden that made it impossible for man to receive and reciprocate God's love was taken over by God Himself,

More books than many libraries could hold have been written on the Atonement, and the different churches are not in complete agreement about how to explain its working. The question of *how* is not of too much importance. The thing that matters for you and me is that somehow God broke the impasse. He gave us a new start by His death on the cross. Each of us now has a chance to attain at-oneness with God and a freedom from incipient schizophrenia—in other words, we are free to return to a state which was as natural as eating and drinking to our first ancestors.

Christ was nailed to the cross, and died in all the agony that the method of execution suggests, but Christians do not regard the Passion as only another human tragedy. It is rather the exhibition in time of a redemptive compassion which is eternal in God. Just as the act of Creation appears in human time as the long-drawn-out process of evolution, so the Crucifixion is the brief impinging on time of what God has always done. By His death on the cross, Christ (who was God incarnate in our human nature) surrendered our nature utterly to the divine will, and thereby united us to God. We have already been given to God. It remains for each of us to assent to the fact.

Christ, as I said earlier, died on the cross one Friday. His body was taken down, buried in a tomb, and the entrance sealed with a large stone. His followers, their hopes crushed and their lives in danger, remained as inconspicuous as possible. Then, on Sunday, the impossible happened.

It is a good idea to remember that the writers of the New Testament were not a poetic group. If anyone is looking for beautiful language and rich imagery, he had much better turn to the Old Testament. The Gospels and Epistles read more like hurried jottings in a diary or the letters that plain people write to one another. The majestic prose of the King James translation is much less majestic when read in the Greek original. So—when the Gospel writers spoke of an empty tomb and Christ rising from the dead on Sunday, they were not trying to compose a moral allegory or describe the coming of spring in symbolic language. They meant what they said. Christ had died, and now He was alive again. He appeared here and there among His scattered disciples. They saw and touched His body. It was not an illusion. He ate with them and talked with them.

The Resurrection of Christ, like His moral teachings, confirmed what men of many races had vaguely felt before His time. They had sensed that death was more like birth than annihilation. Christ showed visibly the destiny of all men. Whether we like it or not, we have to live forever.

Most Americans are victims of wishful thinking. They believe they can avoid immortality, or that—if they must live forever—it will be some sort of "impersonal immortality"—which must mean, if it means anything, that their souls will be swallowed up in an oversoul, and John Smith will no longer know that he is John Smith. The idea that death spells *finis* is a very comfortable one. It means that you can do what you want to while you are alive, and if you are clever enough you can have a very happy time of it, and then die before too many sorrows come your way. Sometimes I wish I could believe it is so, but I am afraid the facts are against it. Whether we like it or not, God has made us to live not seventy years—or the hundred and fifty years that modern medicine may give us—but always.

I have said that the most comfortable theory is that when we die we die. At the same time I think everyone, if he can get beneath his protective veneer of rationalization, will discover that he *wants* to live forever. We have all known times when something we were on the point of attaining—some *blaue Blume* almost within reach—lured us on but we could not get our hands on it. The artist never quite captures in pigments the mist on the mountains; the scientist sees the boundaries of his knowledge dissolving into a random jungle of equations; the lover, even at the height of his ecstasy, is tormented by the feeling that a greater and profounder completeness of love is eluding him. And there are the experiences of childhood—sudden moments of wordless insight when time stands still—that will haunt us to our dying days.

If it seems paradoxical that each of us fears immortality and longs for it at the same time, I am sorry. But you can see the same thing on a simpler level. Everyone has been comfortably settled in a passable niche at some time, and then found himself confronted by a challenging opportunity. The local welfare worker has a chance to go to China and direct a large relief project. He knows all the ropes at home. The mayor calls him by his first name. In China he will know no one. He may accomplish great things there. He may fail utterly. He is taking a big chance if he gives up his comfortable and safe niche. Often he decides to stay where he is. But the same thing that calls him to China is what calls us to immortality. The stakes are higher, once we admit that we are going to live forever, but we were not made to be content with low stakes.

In any case, Christ and Christianity agree that you and I are going to live forever. The sort of life we shall live after death is being determined right now. Every word and thought and deed is quietly shaping our relationship toward God, and some day we shall know what we have decided. Heaven, whatever it may be like, is no figure of speech, and Hell, whatever it may be like, is no figure of speech. (Many Christians also believe in Purgatory. This is not a permanent state for anyone. It is the state into which souls destined for Heaven enter when they need a further period of purification. It is, so to speak, the anteroom of Heaven. The question of Purgatory is hardly crucial. Heaven and Hell are the only alternatives in the long run.)

According to the New Testament, Christ mingled with His disciples a little more than a month after the Resurrection, giving them last-minute instructions for carrying on His work. Then He vanished from their sight—returning, so they believed, to Heaven.

It is noteworthy that no tone of sorrow appears in the New Testament when Christ's Ascension is described. The reason is that His disciples did not believe He had left them in the way a dying relative leaves his kin. Christ was no longer visible to His followers, but they felt Him as near them as they had when He was before their eyes. This was not the sentimental feeling that one sometimes has of the presence of a dead friend. It was more the way you can sense the presence of another person in the same room when the lights are out. Today, more than nineteen hundred years later, Christ is more real, more a living companion and friend, to millions of men than their nearest neighbors or most intimate acquaintances.

His disciples, realizing at last Who had been in their midst, and knowing that He would be with them always and everywhere, turned from rabbits into lions. They set out to convert the world. St. Peter, who had denied Him three times out of cowardice, began the career that ended only with his martyrdom. Scarcely one of the Twelve Apostles died a natural death. If their belief in Christ's continued presence was a group illusion, the illusion lasted all their lives, and gave them and their converts the power to bare their backs to Roman scourges and face wild beasts in the arena without flinching.

Before He left His disciples, Christ established the Church. It is hard for us to think of *the* Church at all when we look at the "religion" page of a large daily and see the variety of denominations competing for our support. To the early Christians, it was a visible as well as an invisible reality, and I think we can be sure today that the One Invisible Church is seen quite clearly by our archenemy whom C. S. Lewis, in *The Screwtape Letters,* so aptly terms "Our Father Below." Even the fragments of the Visible Church, for all their squabbling and human pettiness, have enough underlying unity to frighten and bewilder the atheistic outsider, as I can personally testify.

The Church, as Christ established it, was not an association of virtuous people who met together as a sign of virtue. Nor was it an optional appendage of true religion. It can only be described in words that smack of biology. It was an *organism,* in theological language "the mystical body of Christ." Christ was and is its "head." All Christians are its "members." We are the arms and legs and eyes and noses and everything else that goes to make up a body. Each of us has his unique contribution to make to the whole. The body includes not only the believers who are living at a certain moment in history, but all the faithful departed, and—for all we know—children as yet unborn. The Church is both in time and out of time. In it, as in Christ its founder, time and eternity meet. It is worth noting that nowhere in the New Testament does one read of a solitary Christian. It is always "when two or three" (at least) are met together. Some modern varieties of Christianity have tried to make religion exclusively an individual-to-God and God-to-individual affair, but this can be done only by going in the face of the earliest records of Christianity. Christianity was social from the beginning.

If the Church, the living body of Christ, is an organism, it needs to be nourished. Christ instituted means of nourishment for it and its members. There may be other means. Men who cannot swallow food can be fed intravenously. It may be that people who have never heard of Christ have somehow found their own way (or been guided by God) to establish the right relationship with God, and thereby become a part of the Invisible Church, as God sees it. But for our purpose, the principal sources of nourishment seem to be three: Faith, Baptism, and that central act of Christianity the importance of which is evidenced by the many names it bears—the Lord's Supper, the Eucharist, Holy Communion, the Mass, the Divine Liturgy.

Faith is first of all a matter of loyalty and trust. You turn yourself over to Christ, surrendering your own desires and will to Him. You are the raw materials and He is the master sculptor. This does not mean that you lose individuality. The rough lump of clay, when it emerges from the sculptor's hands, is ten times more individual than before. You give over a natural personality, and receive back a glorified one. Very few people can make this surrender by one act of the will. It is the work of a lifetime, and even by the time of death is seldom wholly accomplished. But we have all known Christians who have gone a very long way in the process, and their personalities are transformed in a way that can only be called heavenly.

Faith means, however, that you have to take the plunge regardless of the consequences. If you are already watching to see what changes are worked in you, you are still garrisoning the inner citadel of pride and egotism, and have not dived in at all. Faith does *not* mean that you become a sort of sponge, passively soaking up whatever God is pleased to shower upon you. The surrender to God is a passionately active thing, and, as God remakes you, you receive new strength and new ability to lead an active life.

Faith involves a technique of prayer, and the attempt to live in accordance with God's will: I almost think in accordance with His nature would be a better way to put it. It is here that morality enters the picture, and with a vengeance. The farther the Christian progresses in his surrender to God, the more detestable his moral failure becomes in his own sight. This is not because he is worse than he was before, but because he is better and can see more clearly how far short he is of what he should be. It is no accident that the greatest saints berate themselves the most bitterly. But drawing closer to God brings more than realization of one's unworthiness. It brings the new source of power that I have mentioned. The virtuous agnostic has to be good with his own limited resources. The Christian can draw on God's power. It is not a case of God punishing the agnostic and rewarding the Christian, but merely of the Christian making it possible for God to help him. No matter how quixotically generous a soldier may be, he can find no way to toss food to his adversary if the latter is inside a concrete pillbox and the only opening is occupied by a machine gun.

Baptism is the act by which a person becomes part of the mystical body of Christ. It is not so much a symbol as an engrafting. When the twig of a particular kind of apple is grafted onto an apple tree, the twig becomes part of the tree and draws life from it. And it never has to be grafted on again. Baptism is once and for all. It is never repeated.

Holy Communion—by whatever name it goes—was the main act of group worship in the early Church, and still occupies this position with the majority of Christians. Even in those churches which celebrate it more rarely, a peculiar seriousness surrounds it, as though something set it apart from any other kind of religious observance. Endless controversy, of course, has enveloped it. Countless treatises have been written to describe what, if anything, happens to the bread and wine when it is consecrated, and when it is eaten and drunk by the communicants. Here we are again close to the unsayable, and any theory, however interesting and helpful it may be, is no more than one of those clumsy attempts to translate an action of God into language that humans can understand. I can only say that in the act of Holy Communion, as in the existence of the Church itself, time and eternity and the finite and the infinite meet. The Christian knows that Christ is everywhere, but in Holy Communion he finds intensified assurance that Christ is as much with him as if the two of them were walking together down the streets of Jerusalem or Chicago. Christ is with him, and Christ is in him, giving him extra strength when he needs it (which is always) and responding a thousandfold to his feeble human love.

Baptism and Holy Communion are recognized as sacraments by all Christians, with the exception of a few groups, of which the Quakers are the best known. Confirmation, penance, holy orders, matrimony, and extreme unction are also regarded as sacraments by the Roman Catholic Church, the

Eastern Orthodox Church, and many members of the Anglican Communion.

The sacraments are "extensions of the Incarnation." They show that in God's eyes the distinction between the "material" and the "spiritual" is not a hard-and-fast one. God created the material world, and can use it for spiritual purposes. Sir William Temple was speaking the plain truth, and expressing a fact of the most far-reaching philosophic implications, when he termed Christianity "avowedly the most materialistic of all religions."

Finally, there is a note of urgency to Christianity. We are all living on borrowed time. Christ promised to take possession of all Creation, though He did not say how or when. The early Christians looked for His physical return to the earth almost any day. They were mistaken about that, but His promise still holds. Eventually He will reign among men, not as the Suffering Christ, but as the Triumphant Christ; not to be crucified, but to be acknowledged everywhere as King and God. That will alter the world in ways that our imagination is powerless to foresee. Meanwhile, we are living in an interim period. The chance of such a final culmination of history in the lifetime of any of us may seem too remote to be worth considering, but someday it will happen, and no one then will be in any doubt as to whether he has already chosen Christ as his Master, or whether he has made another choice, and no one will be in doubt as to the consequences of the choice which was made here on earth.

Chapter 6. THE WORD
CHRISTIANITY AND ITS
VARIED MEANINGS

>>>>>>>>>>>>>>>>>>>>>>>><<<<<<<<<<<<<<<<<<<<<<<

The semanticists have done much to teach us how language is a breeding ground of confusion and misunderstanding. To the loyal Communist, *freedom of the press* means that any "enlightened" group of people is provided with paper and equipment to publish a newspaper, and that the articles it runs tell the truth according to the current directives from Moscow. To the American liberal, *freedom of the press* means that if you can get the money for equipment and if you can get the advertising for current expenses and if you can persuade the A.P. to put you on their list, you are at liberty to start a newspaper, and once it is started you can print almost anything from Pearl Harbor fables to Communist propaganda; the only trick is getting the paper started and making it pay its way. The word *democracy* is another linguistic bone of international contention. To Hitler it was compatible with absolute dictatorship (wasn't he the embodiment of the will of the people?); to the united fronters in the little nations of eastern Europe it is best expressed by a one-ticket ballot, and to many Americans it remains on excellent terms with a lily-white voting list.

The word *Christianity,* once the theological controversies of the first few centuries were settled, had a fairly stable history until a century or two ago. Martin Luther and the Pope might clash over the advisability of selling indulgences, and Zwingli and Luther disagree as to the exact nature of the Lord's Supper, but these were relatively minor differences of interpretation and emphasis. A questionnaire sent to all Christians as late as 1750 would probably have shown a 95 per cent agreement that it is believed by Christians that God the Father created Heaven and earth, that God the Son was made incarnate by God the Holy Ghost, that He suffered on the cross for the sins of mankind, that He rose again from the dead, ascended into Heaven, and will one day judge both the quick and the dead. In other words, the Apostles' Creed was not a subject of debate.

In the last couple of centuries, however, the "Historical Method" has been applied to the Bible, and the "Quest for the Historic Jesus" has been in full swing. In addition, the mood of genial optimism, which prevailed until recently and is still strong in many quarters, engendered a violent distaste for the grimmer doctrines of Christianity, such as Original Sin and Hell. The upshot has been the emergence of a new religion, which calls itself Christianity, although it no longer believes what Christians have always believed.

This newer faith, which I shall call Neo-Christianity to distinguish it from historic Christianity, has never been clearly formulated, since its followers for some reason regard creeds and formal confessions of faith as perversions of the intentions of the "Historic Jesus." They prefer to speak of the "experience" or "spirit" of religion. However, the central difference is that Jesus is no longer regarded by Neo-Christians as both God and man. He is merely a glorified man. This is expressed in many different ways, ranging from saying that He was "the best man that ever lived" to developing the theory that a fortunate combination of chromosomes made Jesus so good a person that God decided to "adopt" Him as His Son and use Him for divine purposes. Sometimes an attempt is made to retain a bit of the old flavor by saying that "Christ was divine, but He was not a deity"—which means, I presume, that He was a very splendid person.

Along with this loss of faith in the Incarnation, there goes a still more emphatic rejection of Original Sin. To the Neo-Christian, man is naturally good, and there has never been a Fall. The process has been just the reverse. We are slowly emerging from a brutish state, and our occasional backsliding is due to the holdover of old prejudices or the influence of environment. The Garden of Eden lies in the future, not the past.

As for Heaven and Hell, some Neo-Christians get rid of Hell but open the gates of Heaven to everyone; in most cases, however, any belief in either place is pretty watery, and is expressed in such vague formulas as "Heaven and Hell are states of mind" or "We have our Heaven and Hell right here on earth."

Few people, I suppose, have really sat up and noticed how complete a religious revolution Neo-Christianity implies. Instead of man being a creature who was good to start with, but who fell, he becomes a being who has been steadily inching his way toward perfection all along. Instead of Heaven and Hell being the two alternatives in every life, they are nothing much of anything. Instead of Christ being both man and God, and His death being the means of reconciling man and God, He is an exceptionally good man who had the misfortune to be put to death unjustly. The Incarnation goes out the window, and the Atonement goes out, too, unless you want to say that when Socrates was compelled to drink the hemlock he, also, was performing an atonement with, say, 60 per cent the efficacy of Christ's.

The assumption is that somehow primitive Christianity became corrupted even before St. Paul wrote his first Epistle. All sorts of superstitious practices and interpretations grew up, we are told, around the simple, lovable teacher of Galilee. Christianity went off the tracks long before the last of the Apostles was dead, and the task of the true believer is to put it back on the tracks and revere Christ for what He was: the unexcelled example of the good life and the peerless teacher of God's truth. Certain ritualistic features of traditional Christianity may be retained, but they are to be understood in a symbolic sense. Baptism is a sign of initiation into a society whose members want to imitate Christ, and Holy Communion is merely a memorial service, like putting a wreath on the grave of a beloved friend.

In a vague way the world that calls itself Christian is aware of the irreconcilable conflict between these two brands of religion, Christianity and Neo-Christianity. In many churches a bitter civil war has raged and still rages. Tempers flare more violently in these internecine wars than in rivalries among denominations.

Now the fact that Neo-Christianity has the prefix *neo* is nothing against it. Truth may be old or it may be new. The really important thing is to recognize that we are dealing with two different religions, and that only one of them can be right.

It is interesting to observe the progress of the "Quest for the Historic Jesus." The favorite "Historic Jesus" of the nineteenth century was Gentle Jesus Meek and Mild—the humanitarian, poetic, suffer-little-children-to-come-unto-me Jesus. He was amply buttressed by quotations from the Bible, particularly the Sermon on the Mount and the more wistful parables. But no sooner was He established in many advanced pulpits than another "Historic Jesus" was discovered by German scholars: the Eschatological Jesus, the blazing-eyed fanatic who cheerfully suffered death upon the cross in the hope of returning to the earth a few weeks later and consigning His enemies to a lurid Hell. This latter Jesus has never been popular in America—perhaps He does not fit in with the easygoing American temperament—but He has the backing of many eminent theologians.

More recently the Marxist Jesus has been discovered. He is a sort of John the Baptist to Karl Marx. The very latest "Historic Jesus" on the market seems to be the Yogi Jesus—the Jesus who is one of a long line of Oriental and European mystics who have sought utter union with God.

It looks a little suspicious. The nineteenth century was a time of general prosperity in America and western Europe, and a time when it was easy to be optimistic about human nature. The Gentle Jesus Meek and Mild was the religious equivalent of the gentle liberals and humanitarians of the day. But the Germans, that passionate people, rejected liberalism, and the Gentle Jesus was too milk-and-water for them. They wanted something more Wagnerian, and found it in the Eschatological Jesus. For the last couple of decades the world has been obsessed with social problems, and one ray of hope has seemed perhaps to come from the U.S.S.R.: what more natural than to see Jesus as the forerunner of Marx? Today, afflicted with war weariness and atomic weariness, many people would like to forget the practical world altogether and merge into God; hence the Yogi Jesus.

People sometimes talk as if the New Testament were written five hundred years after the time of Christ. Actually, the most beetle-browed textual criticism of the present day has found no reason to put the first three Gospels later than the first century A.D. The Gospel According to St. Mark goes back to A.D. 64 or 65, when many of Christ's original disciples were still alive. Some of St. Paul's Epistles were almost certainly written within twenty-five years of the date of the Crucifixion —an interval of no greater duration than the period of time between the death of President Harding and the death of President Franklin Roosevelt.

Since the "Historic Jesuses" have been discovered by concentrating on certain passages in the New Testament and assuming that conflicting passages are old wives' tales inserted either by the naïvely pious or by the Machiavellian St. Paul, it might be worth while, first of all, to take down the Bible, read through the Gospels and Epistles in a relaxed sort of way, and see whether any over-all picture emerges.

The first thing that is clear is this: Whether or not Christ was God, the early Christians thought He was, and that was the point of the whole business to them. If they were merely out to sell the world on ethics, they did not need Christ: the Jewish Law would take care of that. No, the excitement was over something new. God had become man, and by His death had given everyone a new opportunity, so that the long alienation of man from God was at an end. Plenty of ethics was mixed in, but to these early Christians the morality was something that became possible to live up to because Christ had reconciled God and man.

The second thing that emerges with equal clarity is this: Christ fully shared the views of His disciples. He went around forgiving people's sins, though any good Jew knew that only God could forgive sins. He constantly urged everyone He met to repent, but He never showed the slightest impulse to repent anything He Himself had ever done. He said that anyone who had seen Him had seen God. He said He had been in existence before Abraham was born.

It appears, then, that the early Christians and Christ maintained a united front in their insistence that He was God. The only way to set up a contrast between what Christ actually was and what His followers, many of whom had seen Him in the flesh, thought He was, is to say that within twenty-five years of His Crucifixion He had been metamorphized into a sort of Paul Bunyan in the minds of His disciples, and that their fabulous memories of Him are the basis of the New Testament.

If that is the case, what passages in the New Testament are to be believed? The discoverer of the Gentle Jesus says, "The Golden Rule and the Sermon on the Mount." The promoter of the Eschatological Jesus is willing to vouch for the authenticity of all prophecies of destruction, fire, and brimstone. The custodian of the Marxist Jesus will take his stand on the de-

nunciations of the rich. I am less prepared to say how the un-
earthers of the Yogi Jesus will handle their source materials,
for they have not yet established their own school of higher
criticism.

One of these "Historic Jesuses" might be the real, flesh-and-
blood Jesus, but all four of them cannot be. If Jesus was merely
a man, you pay your money and you take your choice: pats on
the head for little children, or fire and brimstone for His enemies, or the dictatorship of the proletariat, or mystical union
with God.

It begins to look as though the New Testament makes sense
only when you assume that Jesus was God—and still is.[1] God
is loving, and would be inclined to pat children on the head;
but He is also a God of Justice, and will not stand any nonsense
from people whose whole lives are a violation of the moral
nature of the universe; and God wants to see His Kingdom
come on earth as it is in Heaven, though He is not so preoccu-

---

[1] I have purposely refrained from mentioning the miracles as proof of
Christ's deity. They are too easy to explain away as mythological additions
to the simple story of His life. I do think they constitute evidence, however. Not the fact that Christ is reported to have performed miracles, but
the *kind* of miracles He performed. If some of His overimaginative followers had made up the miracles out of their own heads, they would have
given us something more picturesque than anything recorded in the
Gospels. We would have had Christ sprouting wings and flitting from
tree to tree, or emerging unharmed from a den of seventy-three tigers.
The miracles of the New Testament ring true, because they seem so
casual. Christ would see a sick man, and heal him. A man died, and
Christ restored him to life. A wedding party ran out of wine; Christ made
some more. Christ became separated from His disciples, and the only
way to reach them was to walk across the water. Almost all the miracles
seem to have resulted from some situation which made them the simplest
solution. I have the feeling that Christ dashed them off without much
conscious effort. He carefully avoided performing miracles to dazzle the
multitude. He did not want the kind of following that expected a sleight-
of-hand show all the time. The Devil failed miserably when he urged
Christ to jump from a great height and land unscathed on His feet (exactly
the sort of miracle that would have been ascribed to Him if the miracles
were folklore).

pied with the organizational details of the program as to lose contact with Himself. If Christ was God, all the various "Historic Jesuses" are true—as far as they go. If He was merely a man, He had a personality badly split three or four different ways, or else one personality was the real one and the rest are fables.

Remember, too, that the Jews of Christ's time were not used to this idea of God suddenly acquiring arms, legs, and the other features of a human body. To them God was God and man was man. The Twelve Apostles were irritatingly slow in waking up to what had happened in their midst. But once they did wake up, they started something that all the emperors of Rome and all the wild life of the zoos were not able to stop.

I have a peculiar feeling that if any of the Christians of the twenty-first century ever read this chapter they will smile tolerantly at the laborious way I have threshed over the whole question of Christ. The fundamental conflict between Christianity and Neo-Christianity will not be solved by the adoption of a face-saving formula which can mean what each side wants it to mean ("Christ is the equivalent of God to us") nor will it be solved by the victory of Neo-Christianity. It will be solved by the disappearance of Neo-Christianity.

The reader must have been struck by the strong similarity between Neo-Christianity and what I have called "Secular Optimism." The two are almost identical. Neo-Christianity is really a sentimental, poetic form of Secular Optimism. As the latter declines in prestige, and its philosophic shallowness becomes clear even to the least alert, Neo-Christianity will wither away with it.

Any shrewd observer, closely studying a representative group of Neo-Christians, can see what is beginning to happen. Year by year a certain number of Neo-Christians drift away from organized religion altogether. They throw themselves into various political and social movements (often movements very admirable in themselves) and cease to trouble themselves with such questions as the nature or existence of God or the meaning of sin and death. Other Neo-Christians, blessed with a deeper religious instinct or a hunger for ultimate answers, think their way through to historic Christianity, and discover to their surprise that not only is it more "emotionally satisfying" (to use the cheap phrase) but that it also hangs together intellectually far better than do the attenuated forms of the faith. Within a century or so we should again have a clear-cut distinction between those who believe in Christ above anything else in the world, and those who have no interest whatever in Him.

The net result may be that the number of names on the church rolls will be smaller a century from now, but that is cause for hope, if the professing Christians make up in conviction for what they lack in statistics. Christians could never have won a plebiscite in the days when they were almost the only seeds of life in the dying Roman Empire.

Chapter 7. THE DISADVANTAGES
OF BEING A CHRISTIAN

>>>>>>>>>>>>>>>>>>>>>>>>><<<<<<<<<<<<<<<<<<<<<<<<

I once saw a shelf of uniformly-bound pamphlets in a college library. Each had been prepared by someone familiar with a particular profession, and was designed to acquaint students beforehand with the headaches as well as the joys of choosing it as his way of life. Any young man toying with the idea of becoming a physician was warned that his sleep would often be interrupted and his income might not reach Wall Street heights, especially if he happened to settle in a poverty-stricken part of the country. The prospective minister was treated to a somber picture of the puritanical restrictions likely to be imposed on his personal habits and those of his wife.

It occurs to me that the prospective Christian deserves similar warning and orientation. I shall endeavor to set down, as succinctly as may be, the disadvantages of being a Christian.

The convert must first of all abandon the illusion of privacy. He has never been alone, of course, but now he must admit to himself that Another is always present. To the introvert this will be a considerable annoyance, and the most extraverted Rotarian may not fancy having companionship in the bath or at other intimate moments.

God's presence is an especial vexation when practical matters are to be decided, and a bit of worldly shrewdness is all
that is needed to leave someone else holding the bag. So many
difficulties can be solved by quietly moving a boundary stone,
or casually spreading a rumor that is not exactly false but is
certain to be taken in a false sense. The agnostic is much better
prepared to meet such everyday problems, for he does not
know that he is never alone. The reasonably good agnostic
can tell himself that no one will ever know this particular deed,
and he will make up for it by a good deed later on. The reasonably good Christian is unhappily certain that Somebody does
know.

Another disadvantage of Christianity is that your deathbed
statement to the gentlemen of the press is likely to lack the
pagan serenity so much admired nowadays. You may be able
to say with a clear conscience that you always paid your taxes,
that you contributed liberally to the Community Chest, organized the scrap paper drive, led the movement to improve the
zoning ordinances, and, so far as you are aware, never wronged
anyone after you reached the age of twenty-one. The Christian's perceptions—unfortunately for the classic perfection of
his last remarks—are sharpened to the point where civic righteousness and fair play are not the only items entered on his
private record. In the very moment of remembering his good
deeds he catches himself falling into the deadliest of all sins
and thinking proudly that not many men in town have de-
served as glowing an obituary as he is sure to get. The Christian
is also uneasily aware not only of the good deeds he has done
and the criminal offenses he has avoided, but also of the things,
many of them very inconspicuous, that he has left undone. He
remembers the times he was so intent on preparing a speech
that he refused to read *Winnie the Pooh* to his children, though
he could somehow have squeezed in the time. He also recalls
the way he trimmed his sails to the wind and pretended to
mock at what he believed when he was with people who

applauded mockery. No wonder, then, that the characteristic deathbed speech of the greatest saints has been the ancient cry, *Lord have mercy*.

The Christian is also painfully conscious of the skeleton in the family closet. He, his wife, his children, and his revered father and mother are all victims of Original Sin—a malady more embarrassing to acknowledge than hereditary syphilis. It is an affliction the permanent effects of which can be eliminated by a proper course of treatment, but science and theology alike are powerless to prevent its transmission to each successive generation.

Original Sin is peculiarly vexatious to the virtuous agnostic when he turns Christian. He has been willing to acknowledge his shortcomings—his adulterous thoughts (or deeds) and his antisocial activities—but he has sternly told himself, "If only I try hard enough I can be perfect." Now he learns that despite all the progress he has made on his own steam, he must call in the best experts and receive a prescribed treatment. And even after he is duly baptized the malady is still with him, and will be with him for all his days on the earth, no matter how virtuous those days may be. It is humiliating to be let off from the lasting consequences of a defect that cannot be eradicated; how much more comfortable to deny the existence of the defect, just as the presence of certain diseases was once passed over in silence in prudish families.

Christianity also dispels the illusion that you can be your own master. No longer can you play the role of the strong silent man, dependent only on your own sources of strength. You are compelled to see your naked self as it is: a bundle of fierce and contradictory impulses, at the mercy of last night's dinner and today's weather. It is no beautiful spectacle. You need help. But you cannot regulate the amount of help. God is no neoclassicist, demanding only a moderate portion of your personality. He is out to get everything. It is true that what you give to Him will be returned to you in better than the original condition, but first you have to give—really give.

If Christianity denies man the illusion that he is a sort of vest-pocket god, it also deprives him of the solace of setting up cozy intermediate loyalties and building a sense of psychological security on them. The husband cannot make his wife the ultimate meaning of life, for that is idolatry. The patriot cannot create a metaphysical absolute out of the state, for that, too, is idolatry. The composer, the poet, and the social worker cannot elevate sonatas, sonnets, and settlement houses to the final meaning of existence, for these also become idols. The nobler the thing your heart is set on, the greater the temptation and peril. It is easy enough to convince the most enthusiastic bricklayer that laying bricks is not the answer to life's deepest questions; it is much harder for the poet to admit to himself that important as his poems are there is something more important still.

The Christian, too, is to live forever. So is everyone else, but the Christian knows it. The result is that he is deprived of the consolation of a tidy view of the world. He cannot tell himself that if he accomplishes such and such and stays out of jail he has sucked the ultimate possibilities out of life. Everything he does is done *sub specie aeternitatis*.

The Christian must always be prepared for conflict with his fellow men. Christ came to bring brotherly love, but also the sword, and the sword has frequently been wielded on the Christian. It is true that the American Christian of the mid-twentieth century is in more danger of being invited to parish teas than of being fed to the lions; his social trials, as I hope to show in the final chapter, are more subtle. But if the convert can escape for a time from the intellectual climate that lies on the land as thick as a London fog; if, for example, he remembers Nazi Germany and what happened to many Christians there; then his present favor with the directors of investment trusts and the governors of states will seem less a part of the order of nature and more an historical accident. Since God is the Christian's master (and He *is* a jealous God) the Christian must be prepared to defy the state and the mob alike if they ever try to take his faith away from him or to impose a social order that makes it impossible for him to live as a Christian.

Finally, every Christian is by definition a missionary. He must be one because he is pledged to love his neighbor as himself, and this demands a willingness on his part to share the most precious thing he possesses: faith in Christ. Being a missionary involves contributing time and money for the conversion of the inhabitants of exotic lands, but it also means seizing on any opportunity for converting your groceryman, your business partner, your mother-in-law, and the casual acquaintance on the train. Practical psychology may often suggest the inadvisability of the frontal attack, but when an opening occurs, it is up to the Christian to make the most of it. All of which leads to the unhappy thought, which anyone can verify from his own observation, that the most effective missionary is the one whose life is a living advertisement for Christianity.

Chapter 8. THE ADVANTAGES OF BEING A CHRISTIAN

>>>>>>>>>>>>>>>>>>>>>>><<<<<<<<<<<<<<<<<<<<<<<<

The first advantage of being a Christian is that it puts an end to make-believe. The agnostic, if he avoids despair, does so at the cost of creating a dream world and turning himself into one of its inhabitants. There is no way to calculate how much energy it requires to maintain the fiction of being completely master of your own life, and of having in yourself the resources to meet any situation and achieve perfection of character by an unaided act of the will. Since no one can make a complete go of this business of playing the strong man who bares his chest to the universe and proclaims, "I am the master of my fate, I am the captain of my soul," the dream world can be kept intact only by a judicious use of rationalization. The man who finds himself unable to live up to his ideals is obliged to blame the stupidity of his parents, the lack of central heating in his childhood home, the evil influence of his seventh-grade teacher, or the baleful results of sexual repression. Anything to avoid recognition of the obvious fact that nobody has either the strength or intelligence to live his own life without assistance.

Christianity makes an end of the pretense. The Christian sees himself for what he is: a being who owes his existence to

75

God, but whose nature is very far removed from human nature as God originally intended it. He knows that he is not a brave soldier, storming the battlements of fate, but a sullen rebel who can never know real happiness or make good use of what powers he does have until he signs the act of capitulation. Man (as he has been since the Fall) is a naughty child, trying to pretend that adults are unreal and that the figures in the dollhouse are real men and women. When he becomes a Christian, he receives the welcome that any father is only too willing to grant to his wayward child; his rebellion is forgiven, and he is home again. The immense energy that he put into pretending to be what he was not, can now flow into creative channels. I am not saying that this process is easy—I think it is literally the hardest thing in the world—but the more completely it is accomplished, the more the tension of an impossible struggle oozes from your spine. And the backdrops and stage props of the fantasy world disappear, leaving the real world in your field of vision.

When the rebel lays down his arms, the consequences are far-reaching. Now that you understand yourself, you are better able to understand other people. You know that you and your neighbor are in the same boat. You feel compassion rather than contempt when you observe him continuing the forlorn attempt to deify himself. If he abandons it, you and he have the comradeship that comes to those who have fought a losing war and been demobilized together. If your neighbor happens to be a very evil man, it may be your duty to sit on the jury that sends him to prison, but even in the moment of voting "guilty" you cannot forget that God is as interested in him as in you, and that your own less spectacular sins may be as obnoxious to God as are the criminal offenses committed by your neighbor. You are required—and enabled—to see in everyone the potentiality for becoming an adopted son of God. This is no cheap sentimentality. Christ was ruthless in His denunciation of evil. He never pretended that an evil man was not really evil. The Christian looks at the people around him and sees them as they are, but he knows that the rapist in the condemned cell is the creation of God, and may yet turn to Him before the executioner arrives. We dare not assume that any given person (no matter how spectacular his crimes) is irrevocably headed for Hell.

Being a Christian extends the boundaries of human sympathy in another way. The great majority of human beings have always believed in some sort of god or gods. The best an agnostic can do is pity such people; frequently his feeling is more contempt than pity, and it becomes another facet of the hard core of pride by which he sustains himself. A Christian is lined up with the great majority, and can feel a real kinship with the Jew, the Mohammedan, the Shintoist, and the followers of all other religions. As a Christian, he believes that his religion is true and completely true, but he does not set up a neat contrast between it and other faiths. He recognizes the latter as gropings after the truth—gropings very likely inspired by the one God—and in some of them he sees a very close approach to The Truth. The real Christian, knowing how much Christianity and Judaism have in common (and also remembering that Jesus was born of a Jewish mother) discovers that he has closer ties with the devout Jew than with the Gentile agnostic.

One of the greatest advantages of Christianity is that it puts things in their proper places and allows one to enjoy them for what they are. During the last few decades a pitiful attempt has been made, by people who no longer believed in anything much, to exalt sex into a religion. No generation has talked more about sex, or enjoyed it less. No sexual relationship, whether marital or extramarital, can long satisfy if the bed is regarded as the altar of a new religion. We are all familiar with the personal tragedies that ensue when too much is demanded of sex. One man deserts his mistress because she forgot to use a deodorant under her arms; a wife sues for divorce on grounds of mental cruelty when her husband refuses to memorize the works of Dr. Marie Stopes. The Christian (even

apart from Christ's strict views on marriage) is less likely to
visit the divorce court, since he takes sex for what it is—
one of the more interesting of God's inventions, and potentially
one of the richest aspects of life—and does not try to make it
into a system of metaphysics.

The same attitude carries over into activities that are com-
monly considered more "spiritual" or "social." The violinist
will still struggle with every ounce of his strength to be
the best violinist in the world, and he will regard his craft
with real awe (rightly so, for his ability comes not from himself but from God), but he will never believe that he has
reached the ultimate meaning of life when he appears on the
most celebrated concert stage in the world, nor will he jump
into the river if his vision of absolute beauty continues to
elude desperate fingers. He knows that whatever expression
of beauty he achieves is his forever, and that he will go on
from where he left off—if not with celestial violins, then
with something better.

The political and social reformer will organize movements
to right injustices and make the world better, and will cheerfully wear himself out attending committee meetings or firing
from barricades. He will not, however, write testaments of
despair when a cabinet change overthrows all that he has so
painfully accomplished, or the map makers draw new lines to
mark his defeat. He knows that no sincere attempt to work toward God's Kingdom is ever lost.

The Christian, to put it briefly, is saved from the sin of
idolatry. Knowing that there is only one Ultimate, he can
throw himself with childlike joy into the struggle to accomplish whatever good he can on earth.

One aspect of Christianity that is peculiarly precious today is that it helps us to overcome our obsession with time.
We live in a world of calendars, watches, time clocks, trains
that leave on the dot, and appointments at 9:15 sharp. The
Christian is still in the world of time, and still needs an accurate
watch, but he is less subject to the jitters. This is partly due

to the fact that he knows he is going to live forever, and that the ratio between his years on earth and his eternity after death cannot even be expressed by a mathematical formula, for the infinitely great cannot be compared with the finite. The freedom from the tyranny of time is produced still more by the sense of unity with God, which grows deeper and more all-pervading as the Christian progresses in his religious life. To some extent, he begins (while still on earth) to live in God's eternity, and time loses its power to crack the whip.

The Christian is also saved from insanity. Bertrand Russell, describing with admirable honesty the "purposeless" world that science, taken alone, offers us, goes on to state the psychological problem of the thoroughgoing materialist:

Amid such a world, if anywhere, our ideals henceforward must find a home. That Man is the product of causes which had no prevision of the end they were achieving; that his origin, his growth, his hopes and fears, his loves and his beliefs, are but the outcome of accidental collocations of atoms; that no fire, no heroism, no intensity of thought and feeling, can preserve an individual life beyond the grave; that all the labours of the ages, all the devotion, all the inspiration, all the noonday brightness of human genius, are destined to extinction in the vast death of the solar system, and that the whole temple of Man's achievement must inevitably be buried beneath the débris of a universe in ruins—all these things, if not quite beyond dispute, are yet so nearly certain, that no philosophy which rejects them can hope to stand. Only within the scaffolding of these truths, only on the firm foundation of unyielding despair, can the soul's habitation henceforth be safely built.[1]

Confronted by such a picture of ultimate futility, the average materialist finds that he can best preserve his sanity by closing his mind to the implications of his belief. Unconsciously he refrains from thinking of the final inanity, and concentrates

[1] Reprinted from pages 47-8 of *Mysticism and Logic* by Bertrand Russell, by permission of the publishers, W. W. Norton & Company, Inc., New York. Copyright, 1929, by the publishers.

instead on the possibilities that lie within the present or the fairly immediate future. He dreams of a society a little less stupid and cruel than that of today. But all the time he is merely evading the final futility. Mankind, as well as the individual, is already under sentence of death. All that is so laboriously accomplished now will end in emptiness.

The more courageous materialists, such as Bertrand Russell, face up to the final futility and build their philosophy on "unyielding despair." The Christian is spared the choice between self-deception and desperate stoicism. He keeps his sanity because the universe makes sense to him. It makes sense because it was created by the Source of all meaning, and that same Source is aware not only of every sparrow that falls but of every thought and deed of every man. Even if the universe "runs down" like a clock and becomes too cold to support life anywhere, the significance remains, for all things are eternal in God, and all men who have ever lived live forever.

The conviction that the universe makes sense means that the Christian is at home anywhere. This does not imply that he automatically knows the local rules of etiquette when he arrives in Siam, or that he will find he can immediately strike up an intimate friendship with members of a Bantu tribe. Differences of custom and background will puzzle him as much as anyone else, and he will feel as much physical terror as anyone else when exposed to strange dangers. But the ultimate loneliness is vanquished. He knows that he is not alone, nor will he ever be. His life is subject to the vicissitudes of all lives, but the most efficient secret police on earth cannot deprive him of the companionship that is his today and will be his for all tomorrows.

Perhaps most important of all, Christianity gives to its followers the assurance that their job is never done. Becoming a Christian is not merely the act of being baptized and joining a church. It is a lifetime work. As the Christian reaches a particular stage in his progress he can look back and see the territory he has covered. But he also looks ahead, and sees a much longer path—a path so long that the farther end fades into a mist which blocks off the view. Christianity promises no easy victories, and the victories that are won have to be sustained and consolidated before new victories can be won. As I write this paragraph I am acutely aware of what I said in the Foreword: "Anyone who wants a more detailed and profound discussion of Christianity must turn to books by veteran Christians." The recent convert can describe from first-hand knowledge only the short stretch of the path that he has personally trod. For the rest, he must rely on what he has learned from those who began the journey long before he realized there was any journey to begin.

Chapter 9. CHRISTIANITY AND SOCIETY

>>>>>>>>>>>>>>>>>>>>>>>> <<<<<<<<<<<<<<<<<<<<<<<<<

There is a popular school of apologetics which advocates Christianity as a bulwark of this or that political system. "Democracy cannot exist without Christianity," runs a typical argument; "therefore, let's all return to Christianity so that we can preserve democracy."

This line of reasoning assumes that democracy is the supreme good, and that all other loyalties should be chosen so as to bolster it up. If African voodooism proved more effective for preserving democracy than is Christianity, then by all means we should practice voodoo.

I think this is turning things wrong side out. The philosophers of the Middle Ages were right when they set theology at the apex of the pyramid of learning. We are right if we place religion at the apex of any pyramid of values—or more exactly, if we regard religion as embracing all values, and judge each particular value by how it fits into the general framework.

Everything from sex to politics, then, is to be judged by whether it is in accord with the religion we believe in. If Christianity is true, the question is not whether Christianity is a useful foundation for democracy, but whether democracy can logically be derived from Christianity.

Now history makes it clear that democracy and Christianity have not always been bedfellows. Christianity has lived with kings, emperors, feudal lords, and presidents, and now shows signs of living with commissars.

On the basis of the record, it might seem that Christianity can live and thrive under any political system. Such is not the case, however, and here we can set up a basic principle: *Christianity cannot and will not live under any state which insists on idolatry.*

The Roman emperors found this out to their grief when they tried to make the early Christians offer sacrifices to the imperial images. Once the issue was bluntly presented, there could be no compromise. Quite logically the emperors persecuted the Christians. With equal logic the Christians went underground or into the arenas to resist the claims of idolatry. There is only one God, and the Christian, as he values his soul, must avoid any dealings with man-made deities.

The problem would be no problem today if it were a simple question of worshiping graven images. Unfortunately, the modern forms of idolatry are more subtle. Instead of a stone idol to adore, men are offered the monolithic state or chosen race. It took the Christians of Germany a long time to wake up to the newer styles in idolatry. When they did, a heartening proportion of them resisted the Nazi doctrines of state and race with no less courage than their fellow saints of the first few centuries of the Christian era. Christianity and Nazism could not survive side by side, for National Socialism demanded complete self-surrender to an absolute, and so does Christianity.

In most of the world the situation is more complicated than it was in Germany. Everywhere there is nationalism, and a tendency to deify the state. But in most of Europe and the New World there survives enough of the old Christian attitude to slow the process down and give the genuine Christians a chance to work for quite a different goal—world brotherhood—without being instantly hustled away to a concentration camp. However, if worst ever came to worst in America, and we made the state or the race into an absolute, Christians here would have the same choice that confronted their brothers in Germany: to become "American Christians" (i.e., no Christians at all), or to trust in God and oppose idolatry with all the courage and intelligence at their command.

If history shows that Christianity can live under any political system that does not compel the worship of idols, there is still the question: Are all ways of government equally desirable (or undesirable) in the light of Christianity, or are some better than others?

If we assume the truth of Christianity, it seems to me that some political and economic systems are much better than others. The best system is the one which takes into account at least four things: (1) *the Fatherhood of God,* (2) *Original Sin,* (3) *the spiritual dangers inherent in wealth,* and (4) *the importance of creative work.*

(1) *The Fatherhood of God* means that each of the more than two billion inhabitants of the earth was created by God, and God is constantly and lovingly aware of his or her existence. Unlike many sociologists and political theorists, God does not talk the language of statistics. It is "John, Henry, and Mary" to Him, not "three persons," or "three semiskilled industrial workers." This suggests that any political system which treats individuals as part of a jellylike mass is wrong. John, Henry, and Mary go to Heaven or Hell as individuals; "the people" or "personnel" have no soul, and no existence save that of a linguistic fiction.

Lest this sound like rugged individualism run wild, I hasten to add that what I say applies with equal force to economic systems that depersonalize the individual and regard him as of value only because he has enough strength or skill to work on the assembly line or perform the other tasks of large-scale production. In America, the government sins less against the infinite worth of each individual than do big business and big industry. There are uncounted factory and mining towns where very rugged individualists, unless checked by labor unions, are happy enough to treat workers as an amorphous mass— "labor supply," "personnel"—we all know the jargon.

(2) *Original Sin* is the answer to any doctrine of the elite. This is one of the reasons for its extreme unpopularity. Almost everyone has a private theory that if a certain group of all-wise and all-benevolent people could be commissioned to run the country, crime waves would cease and the black markets would shut down for lack of customers. Original Sin says to Plato, "Your philosopher-kings, once they were placed in power, would be as susceptible to flattery and love of power as anybody else. No matter how trained the mind is, the heart is corrupt, and the greater the power, the greater the temptation. All power corrupts, and absolute power corrupts absolutely." It would have said exactly the same thing to Hitler who, though he may never have heard of Plato, put his political theories to the test in a rough-and-ready way, and produced as pretty a crop of quarrelsome, vain, and unreliable philosopher-kings as anyone could hope to meet.

That is not all. And here the rub comes for many of us. The doctrine of Original Sin means that the Rousseauists are also wrong. The simple life is no guarantee of virtue. The effects of the Fall of man are not confined to men with a high school education. The shepherd is as much a child of Adam as the Ph.D. The heart of the Polynesian native is as strong a citadel of pride and self-seeking as that of a cartel organizer. The sins of the cartel organizer injure more people, and in that way are more dangerous, but put the Polynesian in a position of equal power and he will be neither better nor worse than the denizen of Wall Street.

At about this point, it appears that the only form of government compatible with Christianity is no government at all.

We must trust to anarchy. But that solution is ruled out—again by Original Sin. Before the Fall, anarchy was possible, because men lived by the law of love. After the Fall, anarchy became a word that at most can only describe a temporary state of affairs. If we had anarchy tomorrow, each person would begin by doing what he wanted to do, which would soon mean doing what he was able to do. By a week after tomorrow, the strong would be ruling the weak. Tyranny would be all the harsher for the abolition of parliaments, courts, and police forces.

It begins to seem that democracy, with its time-honored system of checks and balances (that is to say, democracy of the west European and Anglo-American variety) is backed by the insight of Christianity. Power is too heady a drink to be given in large quantities to any one person or any one group. The more widely it is distributed, the less danger of catastrophe or monstrous injustice. Democracy is not right because men are good, but because they are bad. None of them can be trusted to hold absolute power over their fellows.

Admittedly such a theory of democracy takes away some of the rosy glamour. We cannot hope that the year after next all political corruption will cease, and special interests will close down their lobbies. We can never rest on our oars. Democracy will not take care of itself. Eternal vigilance—and hard work —is the price not only of freedom but of democracy.

The same sober awareness of human nature as it really is provides justification for civic liberties. Freedom of speech, freedom of press, habeas corpus, trial by jury, the prohibition of ex post facto laws—these are rightly built up into social absolutes and surrounded with an aura of the untouchable, for they are additional defenses against the arbitrary self-seeking of power-mad individuals.

So far I have been talking as though democracy, with its checks and balances and civic rights, always worked. It does not. It is possible to go through all the motions of democracy without achieving any effective limitation on the ambitions of the self-seeking. The courts can be enslaved by special groups, and the electorate can be bribed or propagandized into voting against their own legitimate interests. Democracy can become a whitewash for hidden tyranny. If that happens, and all efforts to restore real democracy by peaceful means fail, the time is ripe for revolution. But revolution is the last desperate resort of political surgery, because the violence involved is very likely to produce a new set of evils to replace the old set. This is most of all true of any revolution against the *idea* of democracy. It will almost certainly involve some theory of the naturally virtuous elite, and the new rulers will proceed to order people around with the sublime assurance that they are acting for everyone's good. Whitewashed tyranny will be replaced by unashamed tyranny. Then, when not even lip service is paid to democracy any more, decades or centuries may elapse before the practical experience of a people teaches it that it must make the experiment again.

So far we have been concerned largely with government, as though it constituted the only source of power. Obviously, such an idea would be absurd. In America the amount of *informal power* wielded by the owners of large businesses, factories, and enterprises of all kinds is at least as great as the *formal power* effectively used by the government. At times it is greater, as was the case when the sit-down strike of the packers compelled the decontrol of meat. If the government maintains an attitude of tranquil neutrality toward informal power (in other words, if the government encourages pure *laissez-faire*), big business may easily come to have more practical control over the lives of the average man than the government has. Political democracy turns into an abstraction if the workers can choose only between a handful of factories, all run on similar lines, and all having managements that cooperate unofficially for their own advantage and the workers' disadvantage.

If business grows too powerful, there is no balance. A strong labor-union movement can help right the balance. If this is inadequate, the people must commission the government to step in. Sometimes this can be done by regulation, as in the case of the American railroads. At other times, nationalization is more effective.

The fundamental principle here is that no economic system is ideal in itself. (The attempt to fasten upon such-and-such an economic system as the key to all human activities is another example of man's incurable bent toward idolatry.) The rugged individualist and the equally rugged Communist make the same mistake. They believe that the right economic system will automatically solve all other problems. America and the U.S.S.R. have both been vast laboratory experiments, and have revealed the fallacy of this belief. Until recently *laissez-faire* ran rampant in America, but Utopia did not suddenly appear before our eyes one fine morning. In the U.S.S.R. the Marxists assumed that once all property was nationalized, abuses of power would cease. Unfortunately, they regarded property as original sin in their political theology, and did not realize that the abuses of property are merely expressions of a more deep-seated evil in the human heart. The problem everywhere is not one of economic systems as such, but of ambition and power—power of every kind: political, economic, social. The Marxists took away private property and immediately developed a class of managers and technicians who began to wield as much power as the capitalists had once held, and who were equally arbitrary in their use of the power.

Economic systems, then, are means, not ends. The system that suits conditions in one country may be totally unsuitable in another. This is very likely one reason that Christ failed to provide His followers with a detailed blueprint for the economy of the world: Christianity was founded to last as long as mankind, and mankind is destined to meet a great variety of specific situations which demand varying solutions. The undeveloped countries of Asia, for example, might logically make many kinds of activities into national monopolies, if for no other reason than to avoid control by foreign exploiters, while the more industrialized nations can weigh the advantages of private ownership, co-operatives, regulation, and nationalization—making their decisions in the light of the over-all situation, rather than on the basis of some economic absolute.

Up to this point we have considered two of the fundamental principles which can be derived from Christianity: the Fatherhood of God and Original Sin. We have seen that, in a rough and ready way, democracy shows signs of being able to put these two principles into practice. The right of the individual to participate in the government and the various liberties he is guaranteed by law and custom protect his status as a child of God; the power of labor unions and governmental regulation of industry are additional safeguards against the attempts of big business to treat him as part of an anonymous mass. The same features of democracy are also a bulwark against the social consequences of Original Sin, with its inevitable tendency (if given free reign for expression) to result in the accumulation and abuse of power on the part of a few ambitious men.

These accomplishments of democracy are very real, and very precious, but they are not enough to make society Christian in more than the most elementary sense. The other two principles have not yet been touched on, and their application is essential before we can call any society even halfway Christian.

(3) One of the facts of life most emphatically taught by Christ is the deadly *spiritual dangers inherent in wealth*. Not the dollars and cents per se, but the pride and power that go with them. As a kindness to our fellows, we are obligated to support any movement for evening up differences in income. The desperately poor, whose misery so often tempts them to curse God as well as the rich, would have a better chance to think about important matters and long for something other than a square meal. The rich (and this is just as important) would be less likely to go to Hell, for with a reduced income

they would be less hag-ridden by pride. Any true Christian elected to Congress should vote for higher income taxes on the upper brackets.

If the foregoing analysis of the implications to be derived from the Fatherhood of God, Original Sin, and the perils of wealth is correct, and if we assume that American economy is to remain highly centralized and industrialized, it would appear that socialist England provides the most hopeful model for our consideration. The best program for the next few years would be somewhat as follows: Nationalize or strictly regulate the huge enterprises (particularly those, like certain utilities, which are natural monopolies) while leaving small business and farming in private hands; slap confiscatory taxes on individual incomes after the first twenty or thirty thousand dollars; encourage labor unions as a counterbalance to big business —and at the same time, by education and every other means, cherish and protect the traditional civic liberties and democratic processes. There is no denying that the attempt to create a mixed economy of this sort is equivalent to the juggler's trick of keeping six balls in the air at once, but the attempt must be made. Otherwise we shall fall into the hands of either the knaves or the Communists, and in either case be pushed around "for our own good."

(4) So far I have said nothing about *creative work,* for the simple reason that very few Americans have any chance to know what the term means, and few of them, I fear, would be willing to pay the price involved in finding out.

Christianity says that man was created in the image of God. No literate theologian has ever suggested that Our Father in Heaven has eyes, ears, and a nose like us. Something else is meant. Our minds, feeble and erratic as they are, are at least a pale reflection of the divine mind, and God's joy in Creation is reflected in us. Almost any human being, given the opportunity, finds that he likes to create things. The desire is suppressed in most of us because of the grim requirements of earning a living, but it can be seen at work in children as they model figures of clay or plead for permission to mix the batter for a cake. It is perhaps not too presumptuous to believe that God intends us to co-operate with Him in the work of Creation. Certainly the creative instinct is so deeply implanted in us that we suppress it at our psychological peril.

As life is lived in America today, writers, artists, musicians, and farmers are almost the only adults who have a fighting chance of expressing their creative instinct during the greater part of each day. Bigness has been the death of the creative urge for most of us. The sorrows of the assembly line have been so often rehearsed that I shall not linger long over them here, except to say that if anyone spends a week in Detroit or any other center of mass production he is obliged to vouch for the sober accuracy of everything said against this way of life. It is impossible to feel creative satisfaction when one's task is to screw one part onto the half-completed body of an automobile as it comes to a halt for a carefully calculated number of seconds. It is deadening to the creative instinct to find that maximum efficiency is often reached after three or four weeks of work, and a boy of eighteen is a more efficient worker than his father. No wonder that so many workers in huge plants go home to listen to the cheapest radio programs and read the funnies, or else go out to play the slot machines and bolster their egos with boastful talk over the beer bottles. Their daytime work is subhuman, and their evenings are of a kind.

Any proposal for decentralization and small-scale economy is always met with the inquiry, "Do you want to turn the hands on the clock back? Do you want everybody to live like the mountaineers in *The New Yorker* cartoons?"

It is the familiar "either-or" school of argument. But granting (which I do not) that everyone must either work in a Detroit factory or live in a mountaineer cabin, I can only say from my own observation of both groups of people that the mountaineer leads the more human life, and undeniably has a more enjoyable time of it. Attribute his relative contentment to ignorance, if you will—point out that he has never even heard of electric refrigerators and radios—but the fact remains.

However, I am not such a defeatist as to believe that we must choose between the excessively primitive and the excessively industrialized. A few economists with sufficient individuality not to be swayed by the mania for bigness have pointed out that a great many products are mass-produced, not because they can be turned out more efficiently in huge plants, but because mass production is in the air. Perhaps one third of all the goods produced can be manufactured more efficiently by the assembly-line technique; the remaining two thirds could be as cheaply (or more cheaply) produced in small, decentralized shops, operating more on craft lines and supplying a local market. If inventors turned their attention to it, they could doubtless devise inexpensive machinery for small plants, and tap new sources of power (such as sun power and wind power) for decentralized use. The problem is not one of technical practicality, but of psychology.[1]

If one wanted to indulge in utopian dreams, he could picture a society so set up that small-scale enterprise was deliberately encouraged. Enterprises that of necessity have to be on a large scale (such as railroads) could be nationalized; all other economic activities could be held down to a limit set by law (for example, it could be made illegal to employ more than fifty or a hundred men). The government could employ a permanent corps of experts whose duty would be to develop new techniques and equipment for decentralized industries. It might be found in time that most of the population could live on farms, in villages, and in medium-sized towns, and still enjoy a number of the "modern conveniences" which are so dear to the hearts of all lovers of progress. Any conveniences that had to be sacrificed would be compensated for by the

[1] The advantages of decentralization are brilliantly summarized by Aldous Huxley in his book, *Science, Liberty and Peace* (Harper & Brothers, 1946). Anyone who believes the whole idea is impractical would do well to read this book before making up his mind.

rediscovered joy of creative work: the satisfaction (enjoyed by most of the population instead of a small minority as at present) of seeing a product through from beginning to end, and realizing that one's own hands had given it to the world.

Such a society would have additional values. It would be an effective way of dividing up power. With business reduced to a large number of small enterprises, there would be less need of summoning in a powerful (and potentially tyrannical) government to check the tyranny of business. It would have the further advantage—crucial from the Christian viewpoint —of giving individuals a chance to act as free agents who can make significant moral choices. To take only one example: in a highly urbanized and industrialized society, the virtue of Christian love has to be expressed in large measure through such impersonal agencies as the community chest. Indeed, it is hardly possible to speak of Christian love at all in the case of most contributors, for they give their money either from a cold sense of duty or because they are hounded into making a donation. In a decentralized society, where men had neighbors once more, it would be possible for people to help one another personally, as was once the case when the men from nearby farms assembled to help a farmer erect a new barn.

It may be utopian, at least for the immediate future. The most obvious obstacle is psychological. The assembly-line worker has suppressed his creative instinct so thoroughly that (unconsciously, of course) he revolts at any attempt to bring it back to life. Furthermore, he has been taught by the movies, radio, and popular press that the blessings of modern life are the fruit of mass production, and that if it were not for the assembly line he would sink into discomfort and primitive squalor. He might not have to sacrifice as much as he believes he would, but his fear of being deprived of automobiles, frigidaires, and vacuum cleaners is a powerful conservative force in his thinking.

A second obstacle is the state of the whole world. As long as the threat of war is with us constantly, no nation will be willing to abandon mass production, for the security of each nation seems to depend on the assembly line. Without the modern techniques of production, weapons of offense and defense cannot be turned out in sufficient numbers.

It is possible that the atomic bomb (or rather, the fear of the atomic bomb) will produce a partial decentralization, so as to reduce the number of huge targets. It is a grim way of looking at the future, but it may be that only the terror of wholesale destruction can provide an entering wedge for a saner social and economic system. A more cheerful possibility is that atomic energy may provide cheap power for peaceful purposes and make it less essential for factories to be located close to coal deposits or hydroelectric plants.

There are too many *if's* for anyone to hazard a guess. All we can be sure of is this: the Devil's greatest argument is always the "either-or." If decentralization is not possible this year or next year, unforeseen circumstances may make it possible twenty years from now, and the more we think about the possibilities and practical details now, the better prepared we will be if the chance ever comes along.

Meanwhile, what with the love of luxury and warlike preparations, the best we can hope for during the next few years is encouragement for decentralization wherever it does not interfere with the American Standard of Living or National Defense. Practical possibilities include such developments as the TVA, and special loans and tax adjustments for independent farmers, co-operatives, and small businessmen. And (if the people could be persuaded that the idea was sensible) it might be practical for the national government to subsidize technical research for the benefit of small enterprises.

As I read over what I have just written, I am struck by its somber tone. Where is the optimistic note, the prophecy of the Kingdom of God which should make it unnecessary for one citizen to eye another suspiciously? When will the lion and the lamb lie down together?

It may be that the consummation of the Kingdom of God rests altogether outside of history as we know it—that it will come to pass only when Christ intervenes for the second and final time. But in a sense the Kingdom of God is among us now, as it has been ever since it was established more than nineteen hundred years ago. It exists in the form of the Invisible Church—palely, very palely reflected in the visible fragments of that Church. The Visible Church is always a mixture of good and evil, and at times the evil seems to predominate. It is a hybrid. Its mother is the Invisible Church, which extends into the farthest reaches of time and embraces all who surrender themselves to God as revealed in Christ, but its father is just plain man, with all his selfishness and selfish cunning. The wonder is not that the fragments of the Visible Church are so ineffectual and timid, but that they have as much integrity and vitality as they do.

One reason for the ineffectuality of the Visible Church is that most of the men of good will are not in it. With idealistic but sentimental hearts they have thrown themselves into the wild-goose chase of the earthly and secular paradise. When they finally wake up and recognize their headache for what it is, and when they come to perceive the only source of power that can accomplish good without multiplying evil, they will be ready to return to the Church, outspeak and outvote the stodgy and unimaginative, and restore the Church to its rightful role as critic and spearhead. Already there are signs that the various churches (or at least their more thoughtful communicants) are waking up. Despite all their divisions and lethargy, they did much to bring about a revision of the original United Nations charter, so that it was not completely a blueprint for the dictatorship of the Big Three or Big Four or Big Five. During the recent famine in Europe and Asia the churches, more than any other organized group, were the conscience of a very sleepy country, and helped prod an equally sleepy administration into action. A good example of social action on a local scale was recently provided by the

Council of Churches in Chicago, which went on the warpath against a corrupt school system.

As more men of good will rediscover Christianity, the voice of the churches will become louder. Mistakes will be made, of course, for even men of good will are liable to self-deception and covert ambitions, but at least they will be close to the Source of right thinking and right doing, and the voice of the churches is not likely to be less moral or less intelligent than the voice of political conventions or the voice of the university classroom.

I feel the need for a word of caution at this point. I have spoken as though I expect an influx of secular idealists into the churches. I do expect it, though for another couple of generations it may be only a trickle. What the idealists must guard against is regarding the Church as a *means*. If anyone becomes a Christian and joins a church in the same spirit in which he would become a member of a single-tax association or the S.P.C.A. he has missed the whole point. For the Church to speak with true authority, its members, or at least a respectable number of them, must be real *Christians*. That means a life-long discipline, not a three weeks' confirmation class. It means, I regret to say, a sincere effort to become a *saint*. If the word *saint* offends you, I will paraphrase the idea. It means that first and foremost the convert must struggle, and continue to struggle all his life, to give his life over to God. This is not a figure of speech, but the sober description of the only way of becoming a real Christian. It means yielding so thoroughly to God's will that a new psychological "set" is created, and it becomes possible to do good without knowing that you are doing good.

America has many kind and considerate people, but it suffers from a grave undersupply of saints. If 5 per cent of all church members could become saints, the practical good for the general population would be out of all proportion. The man who has truly established a relation with God, or gone a long way toward it—the man who has permitted God to restore his nature to some semblance of what human nature was at Creation—can have an effect on other people forever beyond the ability of the merely kind and well-intentioned. There is something catching about holiness.

So, I am afraid the social application of Christianity depends even more on you and me than it does on any super-organization of churches or set of pronouncements, desirable and necessary as these are in themselves. There is no short cut. If we want to make society more Christian, we must first become Christians ourselves.

Chapter 10. THE CONVERT AND THE CHALLENGE

>>>>>>>>>>>>>>>>>>>>>><<<<<<<<<<<<<<<<<<<<<<

There are certain questions tnat occur to anyone hovering on the edge of Christianity, and they deserve an honest answer (even though the only honest answer may sound very vague and inconclusive to the questioner).

First of all, how can anyone be certain that Christianity is true? If the word *true* is used as a synonym for "verifiable by objective observation" (as in the statement, "It is true that a ball tossed into the air will fall back to earth"), the answer is that there is no way of proving the truth of Christianity.

In the earlier part of this book I gave the reasons that make me believe it highly probable that Christianity *is* true. Essentially, I started with the assumption that human life has an over-all meaning, and that God is the source of that meaning. I then went on to discuss the main features of Christian theology, and tried to show that they hang together in a remarkable way, so that the whole structure is intellectually, as well as emotionally, satisfying.

Anyone is at perfect liberty to deny my fundamental assumption and say, "As far as I can see, there is no meaning to life." In that case, it is no use trying to discuss the matter further. Any system of geometry is based on a handful of axioms, and the axioms are forever unprovable.

Very rarely is anyone vouchsafed a miracle or vision to produce instant and lasting certainty of the truth of Christianity. Perhaps that is just as well; St. Paul was blind for several days after Christ spoke to him in a vision on the road to Damascus. Most of us are confronted with the necessity of making a decision (a decision of life or death, if Christianity *is* true) without any means of proving beyond doubt that the decision is right. Though we thresh the matter over for thirty years and read every book in the Congressional Library, the final plunge must be an act of faith.

Making the plunge of faith is not like solving an algebra problem; it is like getting married. No mathematical or scientific formula can *prove* that two people ought to live together the rest of their lives. Nor will a careful balancing of pro's and con's—family backgrounds, community of interests, temperament, etc.—provide more than a preliminary basis of consideration. The final decision to go to the altar arises partly from a shrewd balancing of impressions, but much more from a deep-set (but logically unjustifiable) confidence that it is the profoundly right thing to do.

The most happily married couple has spells when the magic and completeness of the relationship seems suspended—days when the man and wife are almost strangers to each other. The saints as well as everyday Christians report similar experiences in their religious life. Even after the plunge of faith is made and all bridges are burned, there are times when the sense of God's presence fades—when He seems to withdraw Himself and leave the soul naked. Doubts and questionings come swarming like a leering army. If we can believe the testimony of the saints, such periods of "spiritual dryness" are not to be feared but rather to be *accepted* and *used*. Provided that the Christian carries on in his daily life as he has been taught by Christ, and prays constantly to the withdrawn God, he will find eventually that God is not withdrawn, that He is more intensely present than before. After a period of dryness comes a new and higher plateau in one's religious life. But the times of aloneness come and go, with most of us, to the very end of life, and any Christian should reckon with them.

Another question—one naturally asked by anyone who has made up his mind to embrace Christianity—is *What church?*

The very fact that such a question has to be asked is a depressing commentary on human nature, with its self-glorification and greed for power. There should be only one Visible Church, as there is only one Invisible Church. The brute fact remains, however; the Visible Church is split into hundreds of fragments, some including millions of communicants, and some confined to a few hundreds. Unless the convert is prepared to make himself into a church with a membership of one, he is obliged to choose among the sprawling assortment of denominations competing for his favor.

The average Christian, I suppose, is quietly convinced that one particular denomination (his own) is a peculiarly accurate embodiment of the Church as Christ established it, and that four or five other denominations (listed in the order of decreasing desirability) are the runners-up. I have such a list in my own mind, but have no intention of committing it to paper here. The consoling thought is that one can choose almost any church and still belong to a society which has much more in common with other Christian groups than it does with the secular world outside. Centuries of division and recrimination have not succeeded in completely destroying the underlying unity and similarity of the various Christian communions.

The tendency to divide and subdivide, which has raged since the Reformation, seems to have spent its force. A slow but strong pull now exists toward the reunion of Christendom. Several large-scale mergers of Protestant denominations have been consummated in the last few decades, and others are in the air. The Anglican Communion and the various branches of the Eastern Orthodox Church are gradually moving toward "intercommunion"—that is, a mutual recognition of the validity of each other's ministry and sacraments. The attempt to re-establish Christian unity should be greatly aided by the gradual disappearance of Neo-Christianity, for with its demise the various denominations will be able to see more clearly how much they hold the same beliefs in common.

However, we are living now, and the unity of Christendom lies far in the future, if it is ever to come to pass. For the present, there is one further fact which should bring some ray of consolation: the fragmentary state of the Visible Church means that each denomination is likely to be especially outstanding in its understanding of certain values of Christianity. The Quakers have their tradition of mystical union with God and their devotion to humanitarian work. The Roman Catholic Church, the Eastern Orthodox Church, and the Anglican Communion have kept a profound appreciation of the sacraments. The Methodist Church has a peculiarly strong sense of the social implications of Christianity. The list could be extended indefinitely. In the utopian future, each denomination may pour into the Church the values it has so lovingly conserved and developed. For the time being, it is a comfort and a hopeful thing that each fragment of the Church has its particular strong points.

I have so far been speaking as though I assumed that every Christian must of necessity belong to some church. What is there to say to the person who states, "I believe in Christ and in everything that Christians have always considered a part of their faith, but I get nothing whatever out of going to church"?

This statement may be made for two different reasons. Sometimes the person is so deeply and genuinely religious that he is appalled by the shallowness and hypocrisy of many congregations and ministers. He may be speaking the honest truth when he says that he has a more profound religious experience watching a sunset from a hillside than singing hymns in a neo-gothic structure. But if that is the case, he is badly needed by some church, to raise its religious level and desecularize its atmosphere. He should belong to a church, even at the risk of complicating his own religious life.

More often, I fear, the statement is a reflection of spiritual pride. Religion, being the most intense experience of life, is also the most dangerous. Nothing is easier than to become convinced that the people around you are less "spiritual" than you are. The pews of every church are filled with semi-Christians, with sinners, with outright hypocrites. So much the more reason for the victim of spiritual pride to take his place in a pew, for by observing his neighbors he may be led to reflect that in their eyes he has as many failings as they have in his.

Whatever one's reasons for trying to be a lone-wolf Christian, the attempt is likely to end in excessive subjectivism or estheticism. The man who goes to a hillside to watch the sunset and think about God very soon begins to go to the hillside to watch the sunset and think about himself watching the sunset. After a time it is probable he will decide that he does not need to go to the hillside. He will stay at home, bathed in the warm afterglow of the self-approbation he stored up during his pilgrimages to the hillside.

One further consideration, which verges on politics, may not be out of place. If the early Christians had not been organized, the Roman emperors would most likely have been able to wipe the movement out at the very beginning. If the Christians of Germany had not belonged to churches, they could have done almost nothing to oppose Hitler, and his plans for paganizing the country would have proceeded much more swiftly. Today, in America, Christians stand in little peril, but they cannot afford to gamble on perpetual security. The Devil always organizes his allies efficiently, and we dare not assume that Christians will forever be immune from a frontal and sanguinary assault.

The greatest psychological problem faced by a Christian today is probably a feeling of excessive respectability. This is particularly so in the case of the convert. Once upon a time he was a daring fellow. He shocked the *bourgeoisie* with his brilliant epigrams, and had the reputation of being quite a bohemian and advanced thinker. Now the sweet old ladies who used to shake their heads over him are all smiles as he enters his pew. If only he had decided on Buddhism or Shinto—then he could be religious and stand out from the herd at the same time!

Christianity, even today, is as familiar as an old shoe. Few people know as much of it as the Apostles' Creed, but everyone has heard of it. The feeling of the utterly commonplace is not lessened by all the Youth-for-Christ posters in store windows, and the flood of cheaply sentimental religious novels.

What the modern convert lacks—and what the first converts had to an exhilarating degree—is the sense of danger. To be a Christian in the Roman Empire under Diocletian was as perilous as to be a Communist in Spain under Franco.

If we could believe that America is on the verge of a tremendous revival and rejuvenation of Christianity, it would be easier to bear the cross of respectability—we could tell ourselves that the seeming alliance with Mrs. Grundy is a short-term affair. As I said earlier, the more optimistic Christians have recently made many prophecies of this sort. I wish I could agree with them, but unless I am completely mistaken in my private analysis of the signs of the times, the renaissance of Christianity lies several generations in the future.

I come to this pessimistic conclusion, first of all, because there are still many frontiers for "Secular Optimism" to cross. The fanatical cultists of the South, who have recently been battling for their constitutional right to handle poisonous serpents, are really survivals of the past. The modern enlightenment has scarcely touched them. Once they are provided with good schools, and newspapers and radios are found in more of their homes, their fanatical religion will begin to fade. They will then be ripe for the gospel of Secular Optimism. All over the South, and to some extent in other parts of the country, there are these cultural pockets which preserve in a dwarfed and hardened form the beliefs of an older day. Much missionary work lies ahead for Secular Optimism. The last snake handler will probably be introduced to the works of H. G. Wells and John Dewey about seventy-five years from now, when the rest of the country is rediscovering a book called the New Testament.

The second reason that I believe Secular Optimism is not headed for immediate extinction is that even two world wars may not be enough to destroy the confidence of the man in the street. This is particularly true in America, which has suffered so much less than most of the globe. The casual assumption on the part of the American civilian that nothing drastic could ever happen to the world is not shaken by anything he reads in the newspapers. It is a belief so deep-seated that returning veterans, who saw the grimmest proof of what can happen, often yield to this mood after a few months and begin to talk as though everything they had seen with their own eyes was an optical illusion.

The gospel of Secular Optimism promises quick returns, and spares its disciples the more painful kinds of soul searching. All they are required to do is behave with a necessary minimum of civic righteousness, be cheerful, and work hard in their laboratories and factories until the first pictures of Utopia appear in the rotogravure section.

Already the more sensitive and intelligent are beginning to see through this figure skating on the surface of life, but they may be generations ahead of their times. The majority of the population, though increasingly troubled in the depths of the subconscious, will very likely continue to figure skate as long as the dinner pail is full and the greatest perils in immediate view are automobiles and cancer.

It may be, of course, that the next couple of centuries will be a prolonged muddle, with no definite changes of a fundamental sort occurring. We may avoid catastrophic wars among large nations, and not be too much affected by small-scale conflicts in remote places. Capital and labor may jockey for power, without either side ever achieving total victory. Utopia may advance and recede with the fluctuating course of events. All this is possible, and if it comes to pass, disillusionment with Secular Optimism will be a slow process. It will come about as individuals here and there grow more mature, and begin to question the philosophic basis of the accepted faith.

It seems more likely, however, that the figure skating will come to a somewhat more abrupt end. It will be brought to a halt by one of two things: catastrophe or success.

The atomic prophets of doom are so numerous nowadays that I need not dwell on that possibility. I will only say that it is a possibility, if not a probability, and that if it occurs the vision of a chromium-plated paradise will quietly fade into folklore as the scattered survivors of the debacle fashion themselves hoes of crooked sticks and try to scratch a little food out of the ground. Any concept of "progress" would be limited to dreams of a golden day when everyone would have a horse and some sort of wheeled contrivance.

If catastrophe does come, the Christians will have exciting work cut out for them. In a world of burnt-out libraries, shattered communications, and leveled factories, what would keep men from one another's throats and make it possible for little villages to spring up and crops to be sown? Not Communism, for it depends on directives from headquarters and the output of tractor factories. Not ethical culture or Neo-Christianity, for they are sunny-weather faiths. Only Christianity has the driving power to save people from despair and teach them to work together and build new foundations for community life. This is not theorizing. The laboratory was the Roman Empire, when the blond barbarians exploded across the frontiers with the impact of an A-bomb.

I do not think catastrophe is inevitable. I would give even odds that somehow the nations will blunder through the present period without blowing one another to bits. Either one world or a semipermanent balance of power may evolve.

Capital and labor may refrain from civil wars. We may actually see the emergence of something approximating the Secular Utopia. A rising standard of living throughout the world, increased leisure, greater justice among individuals and classes—these could all come to pass.

I hope that this second possibility is what actually happens. My reasons are not wholly humanitarian. I should like to see a world in which everyone had a groaning dinner table, worked only four hours a day, and could write sonnets and photograph wild life to his heart's content. Then we would have the acid test. The popular explanation of religion is that it promises "pie in the sky." Give a man pie on earth, and he won't worry about any other kind of pie. Utopia would test that. Unless Christianity is radically wrong in its understanding of human nature, the secular inhabitants of Utopia would soon begin to resemble nothing so much as the patients in an expensive nursing home. They would discuss their ailments, real and imaginary; they would swarm to astrologers and crystal-gazers; subtle forms of sexual perversion and sadism would spread like an epidemic. Anything to relieve the boredom of leading a *merely* human life. In time, the more intelligent would rediscover Christianity, and find out why they were bored. They would pass along their discovery, and then, at last, Utopia would have a chance of being a blessing. Everyone could be properly grateful for food and the other good things of life, and could then concentrate on the important thing, his relation to God.

The Christian of today, troubled by his excessive respectability, can scarcely hope that he will ever be honored with martyrdom. The lack of danger to life and limb does not justify him, however, in sitting back and assuming that he has no challenges to meet. Nor can he daydream about a day when America will be re-Christianized, and the faith of two thousand years suddenly become more a living thing to the masses than the writings of John Dewey and H. G. Wells.

The challenges facing the Christian of today are less spectacular than those that confronted the early Christians, but for that very reason they are perhaps harder to meet. They are imbedded in his day-by-day responsibilities as a citizen.

With all its imperfections, America is a democracy. If our social and economic system is shot through with monstrous injustices, we cannot blame a set of autocratic rulers. We can only blame our own indifference or our own selfishness. The Christian who has completely committed his life to God as revealed in Christ has no choice but to struggle to remake society in the image of Christ. The political machinery exists for translating his will into reality.

Christians—that is, completely committed Christians—are a minority today, and may be a minority for a long time to come, but that does not release them from their categorical obligations to society. They must make up in devotion and intensity for what they lack in numbers. Having given themselves heart and soul to an absolute, they will be able to exercise an influence out of proportion to their numbers on other people who have not reached the point of wholeheartedly embracing Christianity. A little leaven goes a long way.

Unlike the various brands of secularists, the Christian is a realist. He can face setbacks without despair. He will not succeed overnight in establishing the Kingdom of God on earth; indeed, he is aware that its complete consummation probably lies outside history as we know it. But there are as many degrees of good as of evil, and it is always possible to advance from one degree of good to a higher degree. Something closer to the Kingdom of God than mankind has yet seen can be created here in America. The political machinery exists. It is waiting for Christians to use it. The question is: What is the highest purpose for which the technique of democracy can be used?

To the Christian who has committed his life to God, there can be only one answer. The highest purpose of democracy is the same as the loftiest goal in every compartment of human life. It is directed toward the One who created all life and the meaning of all life. The true aim of politics was stated nearly two thousand years ago: Thy will be done, on earth as it is in Heaven.

INDEX